FROM

P.O.W.

TO

C.E.O.

an after–war memoir

LOET VELMANS

VHᴮ

From P.O.W to C.E.O
Copyright © 2015 by Loet Velmans

Book design by Emma Schlieder

Printed in the United States of America

ISBN: 978-0-9835505-1-8

To Edith, for putting up with me for 66 years, Hester, my indispensible editor, and the rest of the members of the Velmans tribe, including those yet to come.

CONTENTS

Introduction

////////////////////////////////////

HOME

Life on the pond is teeming. In an early and sunny dawn I sit behind my desk and glimpse, through the trees and bushes, the glittering surface of the water drawing horizontal stripes of unequal width. Often one fish or another makes a little jump, but it's the birds that provide the entertainment, either in flight, on the water, or in song. Ducks, egrets, gaggles of Canada geese, osprey and great blue heron appear at different times and rarely simultaneously. Gazing out of the kitchen window, I have a clear view of the far side of the pond, where a pair of bald eagles on top of a tall tree throne over the proceedings below. The pond is narrow and shallow and just a mile and a half long. Elsewhere it might be called a lake, but in the Commonwealth of Massachusetts its designation comes with a more low-key term.

We built our house in 1978 as a weekend escape from New York City. It started as a small Cape dwelling. Three renovations and expansions later, keeping pace with our three daughters' succession of boyfriends, followed by husbands and grandchildren, the house has become much too large for just two of us. Yet I experience it as an enduring, though somewhat late, love of mine. Not only is there the pond in the back; in front of the house we have a large, wide open meadow with unobstructed view of a Berkshire mountain ambitiously dubbed Mt. Everett. Every summer the delicious smell of freshly harvested hay wafts over us as we walk through the field. And despite the hunting season, there are plenty of deer in the meadow year round. The newborn foxes flit around come spring. They stay very close to their foxhole; we rarely see the parents. And by the time they have grown into young predators eager to go after their own food supply, they are suddenly gone, departed for unknown destinations.

Each beauty has its opposite, each season its antidote. We live through several less comfortable periods: icy winds and snow accumulations; slippery roads and driveways; electricity blackouts and telephone disruptions. When the trees are bare and snow is on the ground, I'm no longer bothered by the coyotes' nighttime howls or the bullfrog's love song that wakes me up in the summer. Snapping turtles and skunks are also part of the landscape, as is the aeronautical fright of two bats that must have descended through our chimney but appeared to come flying out of our TV set as we were watching a horror movie.

It took me a long time to write my first book, *Long Way Back To The River Kwai, Memories Of World War II*. Now, in my ninety-third year, I find I want to put down in writing the many other memories that were unleashed by that book. Looking back, I can see how my early experiences as

X

a refugee and POW shaped the course of my subsequent life. The horrors and challenges of those years brought me something positive: valuable early exposure to ideas, a cosmopolitan worldview, and the knowledge that I had an innate ability to survive.

I am a bit of a chameleon, feeling at home in many different cultures. After the War, the whole world became my home, and no wonder: having fled to England, and then the Far East, Holland seemed far too small and restrictive upon my return. Before coming to rest here by the pond, my wife Edith and I moved in and out of twenty-three different homes in all, in the Netherlands, the United States, France, Switzerland and England. After a three to six month adjustment to each new environment, we usually blended in without too much of a foreign accent. Visiting places like Stockholm, Prague or Sao Paulo, where I had little or no clue about the local language or culture, strangers would stop me in the street to ask for directions. I had that kind of face.

It is no easy task to assemble so many images, events, impressions and thoughts into a unified shape. Often I get stuck in my past, like the flocks of geese milling about on the newly frozen ice of our pond by the hundreds, not yet ready to leave, and then suddenly, without warning, taking flight.

1

///////////////////////////////////////

ESCAPE ARTIST

Some call me an escape artist. I balk at that characterization since there was nothing deliberate about it, but I can see where it comes from. My near brushes with death, haphazard as they were, began when I was seventeen. On May 15, 1940, the day the Dutch army capitulated to the invading Germans, I fled to England on a small coast guard vessel: my first escape. If I had stayed in Holland, the likelihood that I would have wound up in the German gas chambers was considerable, since less than twenty-five per cent of Dutch Jews survived the War. After drifting unscathed over a minefield (second close call), my 45 fellow escapees and I were taken aboard H.M.S. Venomous, a British destroyer, at that very moment in the sights of a German U-boat that just happened to have run out of torpedoes: the third escape. After a few months in London, my family and I decamped for the Far East just when the German Blitz air raids were starting (no. 4). Off the coast of West Africa we picked up the survivors of a British freighter that was sunk by the German battle ship *Graf Spee* just hours before (no. 5). On the island of Java, as a wobbly recruit in the Dutch East Indian Army in charge of a unit of barely trained soldiers sent out to defend our territory, I was lucky to miss encountering the Japanese invaders (no. 6). I tried going AWOL, driving to the coast to catch the last evacuation ship from the Dutch East Indies, but missed it, only to hear later that it was torpedoed by a Japanese submarine, killing all aboard (no. 7). As a POW slave laborer on the Thailand-Burma "railway of death," I was bivouacked not far from the camps that were decimated by cholera; in three and a half years of Japanese enslavement I overcame starvation, beatings, malaria and dysentery (no. 8). Finally, the Japanese surrender came just hours before the order to kill all POWS went into effect (no. 9).

I was obviously not always conscious of these close calls at the time. I only found out about several of them many years later, while doing the research for my first book. But I can't help speculating that something about that extraordinary sequence of events rubbed off on me: a certain confidence, an unbeatable optimism that stood me in good stead in my later life. Most young people, to be sure, are oblivious of danger and think themselves indestructible; but in my case, having witnessed up close the deaths of fellow prisoners far bigger and stronger than me, something fundamental must have sunk in about survival in the face of difficult, if not impossible circumstances.

I was liberated from prison in Singapore shortly after V-J Day, August 15, 1945. Armed with a high school diploma and an interest in journalism and world affairs, I talked

2

my way into a job in the newsroom of *The Straights Times*. I had always felt an affinity for the Far East, and I could see making a life for myself out there. My interest in all things Oriental had started early, when a distant cousin, Jo Drukker, home on leave from India, regaled me with stories about his job as majordomo to the Maharajah of Mysore. Cousin Jo had led an enviably adventurous life, culminating in his position as secretary, chief of staff and confidant of the Maharajah in the glory days of that kingdom. His tales of glittering palaces, elephants, tiger hunts, lavish jewels and sumptuous gold, left me dreaming of experiencing that world myself some day.

So on our 1940 voyage out to the East Indies after escaping Hitler's Europe, I had fallen in love with the smells, the colors and the cacophony of sounds of that part of the world. The vibrancy of the Orient was such a contrast to the stuffy atmosphere of the Netherlands that I was instantly hooked. Even as a schoolboy, however, I had grown aware of my place in that colonial society. A Dutch expat, I was part of a tiny drop of white in an ocean of darker-skinned natives. We were outnumbered by millions to one; and yet the Europeans had all the power. I had accepted this state of affairs without question at first. It had been this way for over three hundred years, after all. Then, in my last year of school, I'd read Oswald Spengler's *The Decline of the West*, a book that made a lasting impression on me. Could it be true that some time in the future, the West was doomed to submit to the East? It was a question that became all too real when I was captured by the Japanese in 1942; but even years later I never stopped being haunted by the idea that some day the East could come to reign supreme. First it was Japan's hegemony that was of concern; today it is China's growing influence. We know that the population of the East will always outnumber that of the West. Whether that is a determining factor remains to be seen, but I still wonder when the scale of the balance of power between a weakening West and strengthening East will be tipped.

In post-war Singapore the excitement I felt going to work every day in a real newsroom was tempered by anxiety at the rumors making the rounds that Dutch ex-POWs like me were to be re-mobilized and sent back to Java to combat the escalating Indonesian independence movement. My experience of soldiering had hardly been pleasant; I had no desire to re-enlist, or to fight the native Indonesians who had been my friends. And although I loved the East, the East did not agree with me. The malaria I had caught in the jungle kept catching up with me, causing me distressing days and nights of fever and weakness. I was advised by my physician that I would never be rid of the disease unless I returned to a temperate climate. And so I boarded a repatriation ship, the *Alcantara*, bound for the Netherlands.[1]

Back on home turf, ready to make up for five lost years, I enrolled in Amsterdam University's brand-new "Seventh Faculty". I was intrigued by the curriculum, which promised a menu of innovative courses in the political and social sciences. Not all of my years in Japanese captivity had been spent in the jungle; while in Singapore's Changi Jail, I

---

1 If I had waited just a while longer, I might have been cured: Penicillin, which was discovered by Alexander Fleming in 1923, was finally made available and approved for general medical use a few months later.

had attended stimulating courses and lectures as part of a spontaneous, multicultural "university" organized by fellow prisoners who in civilian life had been professors, public servants, philosophers, or even politicians. Here, I thought, was a chance to explore the interests I had developed, first in prison, and later while translating and editing the Dutch broadsheet in Singapore. Besides, I was five to six years older than the majority of the incoming freshmen. I felt my age would put me at a disadvantage if I were to choose a more traditional field of study, such as law or economics.

I started attending the lectures with high hopes, but my enthusiasm soon began to wane. The war had made me an autodidact, and I had had enough experiences to last me a lifetime. I felt these professors weren't teaching me anything new. Jacques Presser, one of the new faculty's professors, made an initial impression. A survivor of the Holocaust, he was a charismatic teacher and author of a book titled *America: from Colony to World Power*. I had always been an Anglophile, and read as much English literature as I could lay my hands on. The war had expanded my admiration to encompass the other side of the Atlantic as well, especially since I felt that I owed my survival to the U.S. role in ending the Pacific war. It was with great anticipation therefore that I dove into Presser's book. But what a disappointment! I found it full of Marxist rhetoric, which immediately irked me, not yet wise enough to understand that even historians have a right to their God-given prejudices. I asked Presser if, as an expert on the subject, he had ever visited America; he replied that he had not, and invited me to tea.

I felt like a fish out of water. Strident socialist theories seemed to be a virtual religion to many of the professors and students; these bored and irritated me. Surely redistribution of wealth wasn't the solution to the world's problems! Lenin's policies had already proved a disaster for the Soviet Union, and had led to Stalin's barbaric rule. I didn't see that the post-war socialist tide sweeping Western Europe was producing a better life for its people either. I had no clue what the right path might be, but this wasn't it. My convictions were confined to what I thought would not work; although I had not attached myself to a specific belief system or subscribed to an established political theory, I knew very well what I did not like and did not want to have happen. I took a very cynical view of nationalism in any form. The waving of the flag, the singing of the national anthem with a hand over one's heart, was fine for others, but not for me. My early experiences had turned me into a bit of a cynic—a non-believer.

It had started early in my teens, when I had spent long summer vacations abroad, in Switzerland, in England and in France. By age seventeen I was multi-lingual in German, Dutch, English and French, and was influenced by the literature of those cultures as well as my own. In the Japanese camps I had made friends with a number of Eurasian, Australian, British, and even two American fellow prisoners. The takeaway was a conviction that transnational friendships were natural to me; I also felt that frontiers between nations had always been, and would always be, a cause of conflict, likely to lead to war. I had become a cosmopolitan long before the words "multi-cultural" or "global" had gained common currency.

At the university, the one class I did feel I was getting something out of was a philosophy course running the gamut from Aristotle to Kierkegaard. But I had trouble concentrating. Sitting on a window ledge, silhouetted against the blue sky, was a young woman industriously taking notes. I knew her slightly. Her name was Edith van Hessen; her older brother, Jules, was once a classmate of mine. He had been killed in the war. My eyes shifted from the lecturer to Edith and back again. I found her very attractive. I was entranced by the gravity of her gaze and the musicality of her voice. But there was something else. We were kindred spirits. She too had had to grow up fast in the three years between finishing high school and starting university. She had lost both parents, a grandmother and a brother in the war. Her experiences in hiding had made her a serious and thoughtful young woman. In the struggle to understand Kant and Kierkegaard, Edith won out. I was starting to fall in love.

I soon found that the girl I was pursuing was not only popular in her sorority, but an athlete to boot. She was the president of the University women's rowing club the year her team won the national university championship. I had to squire her in her official capacity to the Amsterdam Schouwburg theater. There we were, she with a multi-colored sash draped across her shoulder, me in rented white tie and tails, seated in the box more frequently occupied by royalty or government bigwigs. When the national anthem was played we all stood up. As we did so, a girl sitting behind us accidentally dumped the contents of her powder compact all over me, engulfing me in a strongly perfumed

7

cloud of pink dust, to the amusement of the entire audience.

Unlike Edith, I was disconnected from student life. At age 23 I felt a decade older than the others, and completely cut off from them. As a soldier and prisoner I had shared my fate with many others. We had been thrown together, forced to depend on one another whether we liked it or not. Strong bonds were formed. At the University, I found no kindred spirits. None of my fellow students had experienced my tropical hardships. There must have been returning concentration camp survivors among them, but I did not meet any. Perhaps it was just that those who had suffered were as unable or unwilling to talk about it as I was. Edith was the exception.

I was convinced Edith was the girl for me; but she was torn. There was another young man in the picture, and she was having a hard time deciding between us. It was the age-old love triangle—two best friends in love with the same woman. In the last year of her psychology degree, Edith told both of us to take a hike and ran off to New York on a year's student visa to pursue her studies at Columbia University's Teacher's College. Her glowing letters home described a paradise of modernity and affluence in the USA. *"Imagine,"* she wrote, *"there's a restaurant called Howard Johnson's that sells 48 different flavors of ice cream!"* She stayed in New York for nine months – a gestation period that gave her time to work out her feelings for me. I finally sent her an ultimatum: if she returned to Amsterdam and married me, I would find a way to take her back to the America of Howard Johnson's within three years, no matter what it took.

In the meantime I began writing stories and articles, not out of a particular calling to be a writer, but out of a general sense of frustration and lack of fulfillment. One of my stories was published in *Mandril*, a Dutch magazine modeled on *The New Yorker*, famous for featuring avant-garde artists such as the illustrator Lucebert. I wrote a glowing book review in an obscure Jewish journal about the poet Nelly Sachs, a German mystical writer living in Stockholm. Few people in Holland had heard of her. To my surprise I received a letter from the poetess thanking me for my insight. Ten years later Nelly Sachs was awarded the Nobel Prize in Literature.

I grew less conscientious about attending lectures. I did not see the point. My few contacts with fellow students petered out; I wasn't in the mood for drinking or the usual student antics. I made myself go to a Jewish student club, wondering if here I might fit in. The good-looking, smart-ly-dressed leader of the group, acting as host, introduced himself. He asked me how I had survived the war. When I answered that I had been a POW in the Far East, he sniffed and proceeded to ignore me for the rest of the evening. It was my first encounter with the prevailing attitude — that what really counted was the suffering of people in the homeland at the hands of the Nazis. What had happened in the Indies or elsewhere was of little or no consequence. It was a case of one-upmanship; a very human need to declare "my suffering worse than yours." This was to cause great bitterness and resentment among the repatriated Dutch citizens flooding home after Indonesia declared independence from the Netherlands.

I had a Jewish friend, Jedidjah, who wore a skullcap. I didn't know how orthodox he was until one day he invited me to tag along to his synagogue, a tiny square room in an Amsterdam alleyway. I found myself standing forlorn in a group of twenty to thirty bearded and black-hatted men swaying and chanting their Hebrew prayers. It was stuffy in that cramped space, overheated by the ardor of their communal recitations. I felt very alien and most uncomfortable. Later I had to wonder how these Hasidic men had survived, and what agonies they must have suffered. I felt pity for them; strangely enough, I did not identify with their fate. My three and a half years as a prisoner of the Japanese had been a full round of horrors too: starvation, torture, and deadly jungle diseases. I had seen my friends succumb and die. Yet it took several decades before I applied the word "survivor" to myself. If I thought about the war at all, it was about the parts I had been lucky enough to escape: the German occupation, the persecution of the Jews and the gas chambers. Many years later, at the Amsterdam theater where most Dutch Jews had begun their fatal journey to the camps, I found on the commemorative wall the names of twelve members of my immediate family who never returned. Their number represented more than half of my closest relatives. But in those early post-war years, they were not uppermost in my mind. It was the future I focused on; I did not look back.

2

//////////////////////////

AMERICA

Edith and I were married on March 29, 1949. It was time to start a family, to leave behind the rubble and ashes and build a new life for ourselves. Despite the severe housing shortage, we managed to find a two-room garden apartment on the De Lairessestraat in the heart of Amsterdam. It was in the basement, and we soon got used to looking out at the ankles of people passing by. I quit the university and went looking for a job to support us. I had no particular career in mind; all I knew was that I was good with words and could write not only in Dutch, but also French, German and English. I soon found the perfect fit: a small publisher of industrial house journals, corporate reports and the like. I enjoyed the job, which consisted of copyediting as well as supervising the art department. One of the writers and two of the talented artists on staff became good friends of mine. But the best part of the day was when I put on my hat and coat and hastened home, where my bride was waiting for me. A few months later Edith announced she was pregnant. Unbeknownst to us until the day she went into labor, she was carrying twins. When the doctor reported, upon delivering the first full-term baby, that there was another one "still in there", I had to run out and buy another crib, a double pram and armloads of diapers. I was a very proud papa, and when Edith's older cousin Paul asked me enviously how I'd managed to catch up with him so quickly—Paul and Nina already had two children—I deadpanned, "I used carbon paper."

But I hadn't forgotten my promise to Edith. America beckoned. Holland was still in a post-war slump; I found it stifling, too dull, too small and narrow-minded. Edith's sole surviving brother, Guus, lived in America; he had been sent there by his parents before the war to apprentice in the lumber business. He had enlisted in the U.S. Army, and, as a radio operator with the 30th Army Division that landed in Normandy shortly after D-Day, Guus had fought in the Battle of the Bulge and wound up being one of the first to liberate his homeland. After the war he had married a Dutch girl and returned to the U.S., where he was running a black walnut lumber export operation in Baltimore. So Baltimore seemed the logical destination for us.

We took stock of our finances. I had been able to save a little money from my job, but our main capital consisted of the five thousand dollars Edith had inherited, money that was sitting in an American bank account her father had had the foresight to open before the war. My boss at the publishing house promised to take me back if our American venture did not pan out. After settling our taxes and obtaining the necessary visas, we said goodbye to our friends. There was one dissenting voice: our friend Wim

Drees Jr., the son of the long-term Socialist Prime Minister, objected to our going. Dutch citizens, he said, should stay in the Netherlands and not leave; the country needed people like Edith and me for the post-war rebuilding of the nation.[2] To me it sounded like an implied criticism of the United States. My father and very tearful mother came to see us off as we embarked with our twin babies on the SS New Amsterdam, bound for the New World and its gateway—Hoboken, New Jersey.

Suburban Baltimore was a new and strange world. Guus had rented a garden apartment for us, sunny and spacious by Dutch standards. The unpacking of the moving van was observed by a group of friendly neighbors; the number of book boxes in our possession drew much comment. One bystander allowed as how he couldn't understand what anyone would want with so many books. Rich in books, we were lacking in many of the amenities our American neighbors enjoyed, such as a washing machine or vacuum cleaner. For the first few weeks our babies slept in the drawers of a borrowed dresser.

It was in America that I acquired the name I am now known by. In Holland my friends used to call me Lou, short for Louis, but Edith was in the habit of adding a T to the end, as in Lou-tje, the Dutch diminutive, because she didn't like the open sound of "Lou" on its own. When we got to the States, however, we were kindly advised by our new acquaintances that "Lout" meant "oaf"; writing it the way it was pronounced, "Loot", was even worse. So Edith

---

2 Wim would later resign his position as head of the Dutch government's audit office to launch a moderate left-of-center political party.

came up with the compromise: "Loet," pronounced "loot," but minus the unfortunate association.

In Amsterdam my publishing job had led to relationships with some of the largest commercial printing houses in the Netherlands. When they had heard that I was emigrating to the United States, they'd asked me if I would become their American sales representative. The printers had gotten wind of the fact that the U.S. was ripe for the picking. Surely, with its competitive rates and historical craftsmanship, the Dutch printing industry would find a lucrative market over there.

So once Edith and the twins were settled in, I set out for New York to drum up printing business. I'd make the Baltimore to New York trip at the start of the week, returning home on the weekends. I stayed in the Hotel Edison, a dump off Times Square, the cheapest place I could find. It wasn't the glamorous life of smoky jazz joints, glitzy penthouses and nightclubs I knew from the movies. But just wandering in the shadow of the skyscrapers of New Amsterdam was exhilarating enough, reminding me how far I was from Old Amsterdam's narrow cobbled streets. The streets might not exactly be paved with gold, but I felt that here, at least, there was a buzz in the air, a sense of ambition and optimism. New York was all that the box-office hit *On the Town* had promised: it was a helluva a town.

I was surprised at how accessible my prospective customers were. Every cold call I made to New York publishers invariably received a prompt, positive and cordial response. This was my first introduction to the difference between the American and European disposition: the American hearty friendliness versus European reserve. Announcing that I represented a consortium of Dutch printers seeking orders from America, I would ask for a few minutes of the publisher's time to pitch the superior workmanship of the Dutch printing presses. And, I would add, it worked out to their financial advantage as well. It sounded very appealing: we were offering quality work for ridiculously low prices, since the exchange rate heavily favored the dollar. In my presentation I also informed the publishers with pride that it was our own Laurens Koster who had invented the printing press in the fifteenth century, sticking to my guns in the face of the more generally accepted claim that his German contemporary Gutenberg had been first.

I soon found out, however, that it was hard to make an actual sale. There was a big difference between an expression of interest and a purchase. Time of delivery, import duties, and other niggling factors complicated the smooth transactions I was hoping for. In many cases, the clients chose to stick with their domestic suppliers rather than taking a chance on these unknown foreigners. Building trust and relationships would take time, of which I had all too little. Money was tight; we were fast eating into what little capital we had left.

Two Dutch import firms stepped up to lend me office space. The first was a father-and-son general import business. The other specialized in fine paper products from the Netherlands and throat lozenges from Austria. The boss was an acquaintance of my father's; before the war they used to see each other in Amsterdam's Café Scheltema, a popular informal gathering spot for businessmen and journalists. My arrangement with both outfits was that in return for rent-free space I would help out their small staffs with certain clerical duties. The deal was that if I did make a print sale I would pay them a percentage of my commission.

Not long after this, I moved my family to New York. The Baltimore commute just wasn't sustainable. We found an apartment on Hillside Avenue in Queens Village.

As soon as the first orders started coming in, a problem arose. The Dutch printers began to quarrel amongst themselves. They were an informal consortium, and had not worked out a solid agreement beforehand. The lucky printer who won the bid for the very first order roused the jealous ire of his colleagues—competitors in a small market. If I scored another order, who would get it? I did not like being caught in the middle. From my side of the Atlantic, it didn't look as if they would ever get their act together and work out a fair and even-handed formula to handle all the work they were hoping I would be sending their way.

Clearly, this was not going to be the opportunity I had been hoping for. But by a stroke of luck, my disappointing foray into the printing business did open the way to my as-yet unspecified dream of a cutting-edge career: I discovered Public Relations. It happened by chance. One of my printing prospects was a major international oil company that put out reams of glossy brochures and printed materials. I was received by an executive who, I was told, wore several hats. Not only was he in charge of advertising and publications; he was also the in-house Public Relations man. Curious, I asked him what that meant. He explained his role as counsel to management for the company's communications, as well as its relations with its shareholders, the press, government, and other external entities. I was immediately intrigued. I wondered why I had never heard of it before. I did not think the concept even existed in the Netherlands. He replied that he didn't think anyone was doing PR outside the U.S., although it had been gaining a tentative foothold in the U.K.

I was excited. Here, I thought, was a brand new area of business that called on some of the skills I already possessed. It was a field I was determined to explore, convinced I had what it took to bring it back to Europe. But of course I hadn't the foggiest notion when, where or how to go about it.

I had pushed the whole thing to the back of my mind when, by pure serendipity, the opportunity presented itself through the auspices of our friend Leon Lipson. Dorothy Lipson and Edith had met as fellow graduate students in 1948 and become close friends. Her husband Leon, an imposing figure with a deep voice, was a true polyglot, fluent in Hungarian, Russian, and several other languages, including some Dutch. He was then working at Cleary, Gottlieb, Friendly & Ball, an international law firm headquartered in New York.[3]

Through Leon I met his friend and colleague Adam Yarmolinsky, another brilliant intellect. Our discussions ranged widely but usually came back to domestic U.S. politics. I clung to my European point of view, skeptical of my friends' opinion that the American model of democracy

---

3 Leon later wound up as a tenured professor at Yale Law School specializing in Space Law and Soviet Law. As a defender of Soviet dissidents, he and his family spent a year in Moscow in the 1960s, where both he and his wife found themselves being shadowed by agents of the KGB.

was the best model for all emerging post-colonial nations.[4]

One day, Leon told me to hurry over to his office. He had arranged for me to meet George Ball, his boss at the law firm (later Under Secretary of State in the Kennedy and Johnson administrations). Leon had told Ball of a heated discussion we had had the night before, about the territorial dispute between the Netherlands and newly independent Indonesia over Irian Jaya (today West Papua). My basic point was that if the Dutch government had been better at gauging and influencing U.S. public opinion, it could have made a stronger case for itself before the U.N. Security Council, and might have retained some control over the Papuan territory by winning the United States over to its side. Now Ball wanted to meet me. His client, the French government, was facing a similar predicament in Morocco, which was striving for independence from its colonial masters. I don't know what made Ball believe I had any expertise in international affairs, but I must have come off as sufficiently opinionated for him to challenge me to write up an analysis of the Dutch loss for the French. The assignment was worth $200. I was thrilled. I advised Ball's client to be mindful of America's anti-colonial bias. After all, America remembered its own history of shaking off a foreign power all too well. Instead of relying exclusively on the usual diplomatic channels, I wrote, the French should

---

4 Adam would go on to have a distinguished career in government, including serving as Special Assistant to Defense Secretary Robert McNamara. He proved his zeal for the Defense job by parachuting from a military aircraft. On hearing about it, I couldn't reconcile his heroic jump with my impression of him as a nerdy, Woody-Allen type.

conduct a grass-roots campaign to sway public opinion in the United States.

My first foray into Public Relations was also my first lesson in overcoming my personal feelings in carrying out an assignment. My sympathies were with the Moroccans and the Indonesians. My schooldays in the Dutch East Indies were still fresh in my mind, when I'd found myself part of a colonial establishment that took for granted the right to dominate the indigenous population. At home on Java, we'd had a slew of servants living in primitive quarters in the back of our property. At school I had befriended some Indonesians and Eurasians, but outside of school our family socialized only with Europeans. All menial jobs were done by the natives at minimal wages; as a white man, I was entitled to a desk job at a trading company dealing in Indonesia's agricultural and mineral riches as soon as I graduated from high school. Looking back, I realized that the major historic shift taking place at the time had been inevitable. What had given us the right to usurp another nation's wealth and workforce? What right did any nation have to lord it over another people? Aside from the recent events in Europe, my own forebears, I knew, had long been oppressed; historically, Jews had been barred from most occupations in the Netherlands. My ancestors had been cattle dealers, one of the few opportunities open to them besides butchering, peddling, diamond-cutting, money-lending or domestic service.

Putting aside my conflicted feelings, I completed the assignment. My report did reach the desk of the French Minister of Foreign Affairs, but was never acted upon — as I was soon to learn, a fate only too common in the consulting business. Not long afterward, Morocco achieved independence.

This modest start eventually led to my being hired by John Hill, the founder and CEO of the country's number one public relations firm, Hill & Knowlton. At age 60, Hill, who had been one of Senator Robert Taft's PR counselors, was not known for having an international outlook.[5] But as luck would have it, he had recently returned from his first visit to Europe, where he had come up with the idea of expanding his firm's reach abroad. In Paris a member of Ball's law firm told Hill he had just seen a promising piece of work by a young Dutchman in New York with an interest in U.S.-European relations. "Have the kid come and see me," Hill said.

When I walked into Hill's corner office on a high floor of the Empire State Building, I was met by a ruddy-faced, jowl-cheeked, jovial man who shook my hand with a crushing grip. The conversation went well. Hill asked a lot of questions about my background, experience and aspirations. Hill described the interview in his memoir[6] as follows:

> "I was impressed but had not expected to hire anyone immediately, so I thought to discourage him by saying that anyone hired then in our embryo

---

5 In a letter to Leon Lipson of Oct 15, 1952, in which I ask Leon if he knows Edward L. Bernays, I write rather sarcastically, "...who seems to be PR adviser to the Stevenson staff. That stigma should make him more internationally minded than Hill."

6 Hill, John W. *The Making of a Public Relations Man.* New York: David McKay, 1963.

international division would have to come in at a most modest salary. He said, "I am not looking for a big salary. I am looking for a big opportunity."

Apparently the modesty of my demands appealed to Hill's frugal instincts. But it was my naïve candor that won him over.

"So, young man," he drawled. "What do you know about PR?"

"Not much," I replied. "Actually, nothing."

"Good," Hill grinned. "You're hired."

John Hill was, in my eyes, a typical American, quite unlike the reserved Europeans I was used to, or even the East Coast intellectuals I had been meeting through Leon Lipson. A shrewd Midwesterner, Hill had started out as a journalist and built his business by recognizing the need for public outreach on the part of the Midwest's steel industry. His gruff, disarming exterior belied a very keen nose for business, a talent for making connections, and an instinctive knack for being in the right place at the right time. I had no idea what made him decide to give me a chance; maybe it was my knowledge of languages that persuaded him, or my writing ability. The upshot was that I would go to work in his New York office. If my performance was up to par, he'd see about using me for his European plans.

With the prospect of a steady paycheck, I no longer had to worry about the next commission coming through. The printers and I parted on amicable terms, and Edith and I moved to a row house in Parkway Village, Queens, where our twins attended the United Nations Nursery School just around the corner.

Having missed the fun of a carefree youth, I felt I had to make up for lost time. Life in post-war Holland had been dull, grim and serious. The laughter was reserved for our own little family, and just the odd close friend or two. During our first two years in the States we had been living hand to mouth; at one low point I had even resorted to selling Encyclopedia Britannicas to make some extra cash, enlisting Edith to help me in hand-addressing hundreds of mailers to strangers we found in the telephone book. There had been no extra money for luxuries. We were still living on a very tight budget; but now, on our wedding anniversary, we splurged on a fancy night out. Edith looked stunning in what had been her wedding dress, which she had dyed black and shortened to a fashionable "New Look" length; we danced cheek to cheek under a starlit sky in the open-roofed ballroom of the Waldorf Astoria. On another occasion we made a foray into Greenwich Village with our friends Hillel and Aviva, a popular Israeli folk-singing duo we had met through mutual acquaintances. Trailing behind the troubadours as they strolled through the Village in sandals, playing a shepherd's flute, dressed like hippies at least ten years ahead of their time, I surprised myself by not being totally embarrassed. Prison camp had left its mark, however, and made it difficult for me to act young and carefree. As a newly-minted New Yorker, I was learning to appreciate the freedom of the city so vitally alive around me. Yet I was never completely able to shake off the grim, inhibiting grip of my prison years.

3

//////////////////////////////////////

AROUND THE WORLD IN 79 DAYS

In 1953 Hill & Knowlton's suite in the Empire State Building was decorated very simply. Hill's own unpretentious furnishings set the tone. My office was a narrow rectangular room with a small desk, a chair behind it, and another chair in front. It was only slightly larger than a cubicle. I was introduced to five older colleagues, members of the firm's publicity department.

I had expected my first day to be exciting, even glamorous. But like any new hire, I felt awkward and ill at ease. I wanted to fit in, but I couldn't make out what they were talking about. It turned out that the subject was baseball—an American sport I knew nothing about. At lunchtime I trailed along with the "guys" to Toots Shor, a popular sports bar nearby. This, I would learn, was a frequent haunt. The lone female executive in the department, in charge of placing clients' names in women's magazines such as *Good Housekeeping* and *Lady's Home Journal*, was the only one who did not participate in these liquid lunches. Not being much of a drinker myself, I just said I'd have what they were having. I was handed a glass of something on the rocks. It came with a swizzle stick. Choosing to ignore the plastic implement, I took a clumsy sip. Roy Battersby, the head of the department, whose broad Brooklyn-Irish accent would take some time getting used to, made a big show of removing the skewer from my drink. There were chuckles all around; I kicked myself for making such a gauche first impression.

The next day I tagged along to a press conference, my first—the unveiling of a client's latest washing machine model. I thought I should make myself useful. I wound up rearranging several rows of chairs.

Some of my new colleagues went out of their way to make me feel welcome. Will Yolen, a member of the publicity team specializing in news magazines, invited us out to his cabin in the woods north of the city one Sunday. It was our first outing into the countryside since we had lived in New York; we were amazed to see so much riotous nature so close to the city. Our three-year-old twins played with Will's little girl, who grew up to be the children's book author Jane Yolen. Will's own claim to fame was his skill as a kite-flyer, which took him as far afield as India; his kite was even profiled in *The New Yorker's* 'Talk of the Town'.

An early assignment that sticks in my mind was attending a meeting with a group of United Nations officials to discuss the law enforcement problem that had arisen since the international body had moved into its brand-new New York headquarters; specifically, hundreds of unpaid parking tickets. Manhattan's law-abiding citizens were incensed that the foreign diplomats and their staff could claim immunity under the U.N.'s extraterritoriality status, and get away with parking illegally wherever they liked. Hill & Knowlton had to come up with ways the U.N. administration might soothe the public uproar. It was an intractable problem that took decades to get resolved.

When I was asked to come along to a meeting with Jean Monnet, who became the grandfather of a united Europe, I realized Hill was serious about grooming me for a position in Europe. The meeting came about because the U.S. Iron and Steel Institute, Hill & Knowlton's largest and oldest client, had expressed an interest. John Hill had been the Institute's adviser since 1927. It was a political and economic American powerhouse, but held a rather parochial view of the world. Yet now some of its more enlightened members were curious about what was happening in Europe. This had led to the idea of a meeting with Jean Monnet. The encounter took place in a Park Avenue apartment where the visionary French statesman was staying. A discussion of Monnet's dream of a European union led Hill to suggest that obtaining U.S. support for a United Europe might require professional PR advice. I paid close attention to Hill's pitch; he was offering his expertise, but was careful not to give the impression that he was pushing his own firm on Monnet. (Over the next few decades we tried several times to steer the successive Brussels-based EEC bureaucracies in our direction. We were not successful.)

It may have been through Hill's friend and client Paul Hoffman, the longstanding CEO of the Studebaker Motor Company, that John came to know Jean Monnet. Hoffman had spent a couple of years after the war as administrator of the Marshall Plan in Europe, and in that capacity he and Monnet must surely have crossed paths. Studebaker, one of America's most successful automobile manufacturers, was a major client, and H&K management decided I should get to know it better, since it had a considerable presence in Europe. So in 1953 I spent two days in South Bend, Indiana, the company's headquarters. It was my first visit to the Midwest, and I found much there to confirm the prevailing East Coast view of the Midwest: people there were much "nicer" than in Manhattan and, at the same time, clearly rather unsophisticated. My guide was the vice-president for international affairs who, having found out I was Dutch, spent a good deal of time telling me about his favorite European hotels and restaurants. He also made it clear that Studebaker in Europe needed no public relations help, and that he had the press over there eating out of his hand.

December 1953, my first Christmas at Hill & Knowlton, marked two historic events: one internal, only of significance to the company's employees; the other a decision that was to haunt the firm's reputation for decades to come. At that year's annual Christmas party, I noticed that John Hill, Bert Goss and Dick Darrow, the three top bosses, had suddenly disappeared. We later learned that they had been summoned to a crisis meeting with the heads of the four main tobacco companies. In their absence several staff members, male and female, went a little wild. There was some hard drinking and some lewd behavior. When Hill heard the next day how some of his employees had comported themselves, he was furious. He declared that there would be no more H&K Christmas parties. From that year on, an amount equal to the cost of the canceled party was donated to the John W. Hill Foundation, which went towards supporting the college costs of the children of company employees.

As a junior employee I had no idea what had gone on behind closed doors in that meeting with the tobacco honchos. A major scientific report had just been released for the first time linking cigarette smoking to lung cancer. The news delivered a major shock to the public at large—almost everyone smoked in those days—and presented a crisis of the first order to the cigarette manufacturers. Hill & Knowlton's advice to the tobacco industry was that it should set up its own research arm—The Tobacco Industry Research Council (TIRC). The idea was that a genuine scientific effort would be made to gain an in-depth understanding of lung cancer and of the effects of smoking on the body. My own naïve take on it at the time was that an honest attempt was being made to uncover the real story; let the chips fall where they may. Little did I know how contentious the issue would come to be, and how long the tobacco industry would resist admitting there was a problem.

After some months of following people around and being shown the ropes, I was called into Hill's office. He outlined what my first serious assignment would be. My mouth fell open. I was being sent on a six-nation tour of Bahrain, Ceylon (Sri Lanka), India, Indonesia, the Philippines and Japan on behalf of Caltex, a major oil company client. Merrick Jackson, a veteran Hill & Knowlton staff member who edited the Steel Institute's magazine, was to be the other member of the team. Our job was to conduct an audit to determine how Caltex's various subsidiaries in the Middle and Far East were implementing company public relations policies in view of growing nationalist tensions throughout the region.

I was completely floored, but also flattered. Who would have thought that I, the newest and youngest kid on the block, would be entrusted so soon with such a major responsibility! In Hill & Knowlton's nearly thirty-year history, Hill told me, this was the firm's first multinational assignment overseas.

The duration of the project would be three months. Did I think I could leave my family for that long? I didn't foresee a big problem, I said, but I would need to check with Edith, of course. I did have one important reservation, however. I couldn't see myself going to Tokyo, I told Hill. How could I sit in a room face to face with men who only seven short years ago could have been the ones beating me or starving me to death? Simply put: I hated my former jailers with a vengeance, I told him, and I didn't know how I'd handle it if I had to see them again.

"You're a bigger man than you think you are," was Hill's dry and not very comforting retort. It struck a nerve. I didn't like to think of myself as a wimp. After all, this was years before PTSD would have been a pardonable excuse for my hesitation. Hill gave me one night to talk it over with Edith before giving him my answer.

At home, Edith, as I had expected, kept her cool when she heard the news. I worried how she would cope for three months on her own with two demanding toddlers. But her decision was firm, and final: I should go. I must not let this chance of a lifetime pass us by.

Merrick too faced a difficult decision; he had been about to embark on a honeymoon with his much younger bride.

But he was a loyal company man, and business came first. The next day, the three of us met in Hill's office. I had no idea how ill equipped we were for such an assignment. Merrick had never set foot outside the USA; as for me, in spite of my war experience in Asia, I knew very little about the Middle East, the Indian Sub-Continent or the Philippines. I had kept up with developments in Indonesia and Japan, but like the American ambassadors who owed their appointments to bankrolling the winning party in a national election, often with nary a clue about the country to which they were being sent, I was going to have to wing it.

Merrick and I spent a few days at the Caltex New York headquarters to absorb the client's activities and strategies in the countries we were to visit. If I was expecting to be briefed with in-depth political or economic background information, I was sorely disappointed. I did not learn anything that I had not already read in *The New York Times, Time Magazine* or *The Economist.* What I did come away with, however, was an enlightening encounter with a Caltex vice-president. He examined my business card for a long time, finally asking point blank if I was Jewish. "I am," I admitted. Even though I never denied or hid my religious affiliation, ever since arriving in the U.S. I had had the distinct impression that it was best not to trumpet it, in the prevailing, barely acknowledged, yet palpable anti-Semitic climate. I could not help noticing that the staff at Hill & Knowlton was largely white, Anglo-Saxon, Christian, and male. The executive, whose name was Shapiro, grinned ruefully. "I too," he said, "am the token Jew around here." I remembered that my friend Jay, a former Japanese language specialist in General MacArthur's army, was being given the same "token" treatment at one of the city's largest banks.

We were about a week into our briefing sessions when Hill called us back to his office. He glared at us, peeved. "Can't you boys make a less namby-pamby impression over there?" he chided us. I realized I must have been coming across as more deferential in the Caltex meetings than I'd intended. To tell the truth, I was rather intimidated by the oilmen. They were, to me, a new and alien breed: tall, loud and broad-shouldered like John Wayne, except that they wore a business suit instead of a gun holster. They were all from Texas or Oklahoma, places I only knew from the cowboy movies of my boyhood. I realized that Hill was coaching me to assume the self-assured, professional face befitting an independent consultant. It was a lesson I took to heart. I might be new at this, but I was determined not to let it show from now on.

I kissed Edith goodbye at Idlewild Aiport and boarded a commercial airliner. Aside from a short trip to Europe to meet Hill's European contacts, flying was a new experience for me; until now my ocean crossings had been by ship. Being fussed over by the stewardesses in the first class cabin was now my prerogative as an American businessman. I could get used to this, I thought, sipping my glass of complimentary champagne. I realized that we were truly the proverbial innocents abroad, however, on arriving in London, where we had to transfer to a flight to Bahrain, our first stop. The BOAC ground staff steward who met us and guided us through the airport was a former RAF gunner with an impressive walrus mustache. He insisted on carrying our briefcases. Merrick just couldn't get over it. He had never before in his life been treated with such deferential, un-American servitude.

Upon arrival at our hotel in Bahrain, we found urgent messages from two Aramco employees based in nearby Saudi Arabia. They had left word that they would come the next day for our respective meetings, "as arranged". Aramco (Arabian American Oil Company) was not our client. We had never heard of either of these guys, and there was nothing in our brief about meeting with executives from another company. We were soon enlightened by our Caltex host. Saudi Arabia had strict laws against the consumption of alcohol, whereas the regime in neighboring Bahrain was more tolerant. American oilmen working in Saudi Arabia therefore made it their business to find out the names of any Western executives stopping in Bahrain. It seemed that the black market bathtub gin you could get in Saudi Arabia was so inferior to Beefeater or Gordon's that they couldn't wait to get out of Riyadh on any pretext. Our names had simply been picked out of a hat, to provide them with bogus "appointments" as an excuse for a drinking spree. That was the last we heard from them.

Our interviews with management and staff followed the same pattern as the one that had been set in New York, i.e., we were given the company line, which consisted of largely superficial information. But in this new, exotic environment, I felt energized; I was eager to sniff around a bit independently. Arrangements were made for us to meet with a group of Arab oilfield workers on our own, without any Caltex executives present. The workers' front man spoke reasonably good English. He immediately started yelling at us excitedly, egged on by his belligerent and indignant coworkers. Their grievance against their American and British bosses, in a nutshell, was that they were being forced to work under slave labor conditions. The heated exchange took me back to an alarming confrontation that had taken place a decade earlier, in Thailand, when our group of POWs, pushed to the limit on the fourth day of a brutal forced march through the jungle, had turned vehemently on our Japanese guards. Although the situation here was very different, the sight of these excitable workers waving their fists in the air was unnerving. Merrick, too, told me afterwards that he had been worried, and had felt most uncomfortable in their midst. The spokesman demanded that we relay their complaints to Caltex's top brass in New York. When we reported back to the Bahrain oil executives, they dismissed our concerns. There's nothing to worry about, they said: it's all under control.

A visit to the Bedouins in another part of the desert was arranged for us, I think, to prove to us that the natives were not entirely restless. We were welcomed like VIPs into an elaborately carpeted tent by the Bedouin chief, and with much fanfare offered a taste of the tribe's ultimate delicacy: a sheep's eye. Hiding my revulsion as best I could, I gulped down the slimy thing, pretending to enjoy it, although I doubt that I had convinced our hosts it was sincere.

We also paid a courtesy call on Sir Charles Belgrave, the economic advisor to the Emir. He had been operating in Bahrain since the 1920s as the island's de facto prime minister, and was largely responsible not only for modernizing the state but also for paving the way to the discovery of oil in 1932, putting Bahrain ahead of the other Gulf States in oil exploration. When we told him what had happened at our meeting with the workers, he too was dismissive of our concerns. We tried to engage him, but he remained evasive about what turned out to be a highly volatile situation. Unruffled and painstakingly polite, he insisted on showing us his well-kept flower gardens, his pride and joy, blooming in the middle of the barren desert. Little did we know that just two years later, a general strike involving 30,000 protesters—including nine thousand oil workers — would clamor for Belgrave's ouster. Several people were killed in the riots, and six months later Belgrave was to leave the island and his gardens for good.

Our next stop was Ceylon (Sri Lanka). It was the only newly independent country on our itinerary that did not seem to be posing a nationalist threat to the oil industry. Colombo was a leafy, pleasant city; with its echoes of a mixed Portuguese, Dutch and British colonial past, it reminded me of Jakarta. Neither the Caltex management nor the strongly anti-Communist government insiders we interviewed alerted us to any problems there, although we did find quite a bit of left-wing opposition among students and labor unions. The deadly conflict between the government and the separatist Tamil Tigers, which among other things imperiled the oil installations, erupted much later. We were pleased to report that even though we found strong anti-British sentiment there, the Ceylonese were tolerant of America; the company might want to "mobilize favorable sentiment" for its activities through more active public outreach.

We stayed just a few days in Ceylon; the last day was for sightseeing. The driver of the car that was put at our disposal was an excellent guide. He drove us to Kandy, home of the Buddhist Temple of the Tooth. It was a lovely hill town that had been the headquarters of Lord Mountbatten's South East Asia Command during World War II. I was interested in having a look around, since the memory of Mountbatten's address to the POWs after liberation was still fresh in my mind. One week after Japan's surrender, Mountbatten, the Supreme Allied Commander, a tall, imposing, aristocratic Englishman, had stood on a soapbox outside Singapore's Changi Jail where we had been held prisoner, and in loud, patrician tones, without the aid of a microphone, proclaimed to us that justice would be done. Our Japanese guards and their masters would have to answer for their war crimes. I was certainly not the only former prisoner of war to be frustrated and dismayed, eight years later, at the paltry number of sentences, convictions or death penalties meted out to our jailers.

We found the situation in India, our next stop, more disquieting. The British had ordered the partition of the country into Hindu and Muslim states just six years earlier, and the bitterness of the conflict, with its mass migrations and slaughter of millions, was still fresh in the minds of all, irrespective of religion. Visiting Bombay and New Delhi, the Hindus we met described the Pakistanis as unreliable, vicious and dangerous. The role the British had played in the subcontinent's division was deeply resented; but America, too, was regarded with suspicion.

At home in Parkway Village, Edith and I had befriended

an Indian couple, the Tampis; our children were the same age. Mrs. Tampi was a member of the Menon family, a politically prominent clan of Brahmins who held leading posts in India's Congress Party, the largest parliamentary faction. Mrs. Tampi's father was the Indian ambassador to Moscow. Krishna Menon, the family patriarch, was according to *Time Magazine* the second most powerful man in India, after Nehru; a prickly, resentful foe of American and British imperialism, and architect of India's new foreign policy of non-alignment. In New Delhi the extended Menon family, alerted to my visit, gave us a warm welcome, embracing me as a long lost son. When the conversation turned to politics, I was surprised at the vehemence expressed against Pakistan and its people. Here I saw wounds that could not easily be healed; the seeds of mutual animosity had been planted long ago, and promised an unending and enduring conflict. This was subsequently confirmed to me when we met with Abe Rosenthal, the young New Delhi correspondent of *The New York Times*, who struck me as an unusually bright and insightful source.[7] He corroborated our views on the ominous consequences of partition.

My relationship with Merrick Jackson was never strained. He was an amiable and stimulating traveling companion. He was at least ten years older than me; even so, I found myself being the spokesman for our two-man team, although a reluctant one at first. I would take the lead, ask the questions and lead the dialogue with our interlocutors. Merrick performed the silent but essential part of note-

---

7 Rosenthal was named executive editor of *The New York Times* in 1977.

taker and reliable sounding board. There was a deep cultural divide between us, as I was to find with many of my American friends, colleagues and other contacts. Merrick was a typical Midwesterner: friendly, unworldly, shy, a bit naïve, wide-eyed with wonder. I was less easily intimidated. During this whole trip I felt energized, especially in India. I had come into my element; I had an immediate sense of understanding and empathy with the Indians we met— officials in government, the press, and businessmen both within and outside the oil industry.

On to Indonesia. I was curious to see what had become of the country my family and I had fled to at the start of the war, when it was still a Dutch colony. Now it was an independent nation. At Customs we were ordered to surrender our passports. My Dutch document, with its American and Indonesian visas, was closely inspected. I nervously waited for what seemed an eternity before I was finally granted a temporary permit granting me a short stay.

Jakarta was still the city I remembered from my teenage years. The streets looked dirtier, many buildings were dilapidated, and the place was generally more rundown; but I was immediately overwhelmed with the familiarity of the humid, tropical smell, the deafening noise level, the colorful sarongs and the wide, friendly Javanese smiles. The women were still doing their laundry in the Ciliwung River that cut through the heart of the city, and the stench of floating garbage still mingled with the spicy aromas wafting from the food vendors' stalls. In a taxi ride around town I found our old home. On the outside it had not changed, but I could not go in: like many of the colonial-era villas, it was now a government building.

In Indonesia we met with government officials, journalists, American diplomats, lawyers, doctors, university professors, a hospital director, a police commissioner and European and Indonesian Caltex workers and executives. One of the many meetings that had been arranged for us was with a member of parliament. Our host received us graciously in his home. He had invited a colleague parliamentarian to attend as well. Both spoke reasonably good English. At one point in our conversation, I asked them how secure they thought foreign oil investments were in their country. An awkward silence followed. I had hit a nerve. The two politicians put their heads together. They were conferring in Dutch! Not realizing that Dutch was my mother tongue, they blithely deliberated how best to deflect my question with a suitably non-committal reply. I grew more and more uncomfortable. I imagined myself under arrest, my Dutch passport confiscated. After all, this was a nation that still nursed hostile resentment toward its former colonial masters. Fortunately my hosts assumed I was American. They finally assured us warmly that their government would always safeguard foreign interests, and that there were no plans for nationalization. We parted on excellent terms.

We stayed at a transformed *Hotel de Indes,* where I had first been introduced to the Sunday *rijsttafel,* or rice-table—the elaborate colonial smorgasbord of over fifty dishes. The hotel had changed its name and was now part of an international chain. The food in the hotel was disappointingly uninspired and bland. I asked around: where could I find a restaurant that served the traditional *rijsstafel?* I wanted to introduce Merrick to this blowout spread and indulge my own nostalgia for such a repast. Neither the concierge in our hotel nor any other of our Indonesian contacts was able to help. Finally an elderly Javanese Caltex man provided us with a name and an address, but no telephone number. After a long cab ride far from the center, we arrived at what from the outside looked like an old colonial home. Inside was a spacious, impeccably clean room where bare-footed, turban-clad waiters dressed in crisp white uniforms offered us a genuine, old-fashioned Dutch-East Indies banquet. The headwaiter told us that the restaurant's former owner, a Dutchman, had left his entire estate, including the restaurant, to the staff, with the proviso that he would take it all back if his high standards were not maintained. The kitchen and wait staff, convinced their former master had the power to carry out his threat, continued to run the place as he had dictated.

From Jakarta we flew to the Caltex refinery in Southern Sumatra, where we had to make an assessment of the company's relations with the oil workers. On my second day, however, I spiked a burning fever. The resident physician, upon learning of my history with malaria, decided that I must have been re-infected. The malaria I had caught as a POW working on the Burma Railroad had left me susceptible to catching it again, he said, whenever I found myself in a similar climate. The refinery's manager, reluctant to have a sick visitor on his hands, immediately got rid of us by putting the company's turboprop at our disposal to fly us to Manila, our next planned stop.

When we landed in the Philippines an ambulance drove me to the main hospital. I stayed there for three full days. Soon after my admittance I called Edith to reassure her that I was going to be all right; I seemed to be shaking off the fever. I also told her that the hospital made me miss her more than ever, since my bed came equipped with a roll-out cot intended for the patient's spouse. It was a pity, I said, that this considerate (and rather suggestive) expression of Filipino care should go unexploited. On my third day in the hospital, my doctor reported that the tests for malaria had come out negative, and that since the fever had subsided, I could be discharged. He opined that I had a mild form of non-contagious hepatitis and could resume all normal activities. (On my return to New York it took me some time to locate a tropical disease specialist who, after more tests, decided that there was conclusive evidence of neither malaria nor hepatitis. He said that for a definitive opinion I would have to wait for the autopsy. At age 92, I am still waiting.)

After conducting a number of interviews solo, Merrick flew on to Tokyo ahead of me. Although he had not come up with any troubling findings, and judged everything in Manila to be under control, I came away with a somewhat different perspective. The night before I left I had dinner with two journalists who told me everyone in Manila could be bought for a price, and that by their reckoning the country was one of the most, if not *the* most corrupt in the world. I duly noted that fact in my report.

It wasn't until Tokyo that I truly began to feel homesick. In the other countries we had visited, I had felt stimulated by the exotic locale and the friendly, cooperative people I met there. Tokyo, the final leg of our journey, was another matter. The U.S. occupation of Japan had ended just a scant year before, and there were reminders of the war everywhere: in the bombed-out buildings, the slow, messy reconstruction, the somber mood, and the wary, demoralized attitude of the people we were meeting. Of course this was colored by my own discomfort: everywhere I went I imagined encountering, if not one of my former jailers, at least someone who had condoned what they had done, or shared their contempt for Western soldiers like me who had had the effrontery to surrender instead of committing honorable suicide. I eyed every man I met with suspicion, from the obsequiously bowing hotel receptionist to the maimed war veteran in the street thrusting his begging bowl at me. Still weak from my bout of fever, I felt ill at ease in the meetings with Japanese officials and company executives. They were punctiliously polite but inscrutable, evincing very little interest in what we had to say and offering very little in return. Any one of them could easily have been one of the stone-faced officers I had watched meting out brutal punishments and shouting harsh commands. I was grateful, in a way, for my chameleon state, my ability to pass under the radar; I was not ready to confront, to accuse, or even to admit I had taken part in the Pacific war.

In the middle of one meeting I was called to the telephone: an urgent call from Edith. I nervously went to an adjacent office, thinking something terrible must have happened to her or the twins. However, the subject of the call was more banal. The twins had outgrown their cots and needed new beds. The salesman at the department store had strongly recommended that she purchase them on the installment plan. We had always paid in cash for our sparse belongings. What did I think she should do? As a thrifty Dutchman I nixed the idea of the installment plan. This call, meanwhile, was costing a fortune!

We had been away almost three months, and now we were about to embark on the last six-and-a-half thousand miles of our 31,000-mile trip. Our last night was spent in the first class Pan Am lounge of Tokyo's Haneda airport. The small room was crowded with rambunctious American expatriates and business visitors like us; Japan was not yet a tourist destination. Everybody had a drink or two, or three, and the place was rowdy with laughter. It was the first sign of camaraderie, even of friendliness, I had seen in days. The post-war chill and physical damage to Tokyo's city center had been reflected in the faces of my Japanese interlocutors. The mood had been somber, the faces empty of smiles. Here, in this lounge, I sensed that the U.S.-bound travelers were overcompensating for the Japanese gloom. Among their own kind they could finally let down their guard with loud hilarity and free-flowing alcohol.

I swear I am never returning to this country, and I don't need to meet another Japanese as long as I live, I said to Merrick.

4

///////////////////////////////////

PARIS IN THE FIFTIES

After just four short years in the U.S., we were headed back
to Europe. Over the objections of some other board members, who deemed me too inexperienced (as I was later to
find out), John Hill had decided I would be the man to
gain a foothold for the firm in Europe. I was handed four
Cunard Line tickets by H&K's travel department. As part
of my undocumented employment arrangement, our transatlantic voyage on the *Queen Elizabeth* was booked in first
class. It hadn't even been a point of negotiation. Although
as a relatively new employee my salary was modest, American corporate protocol required keeping up appearances.
And so we found ourselves sitting in the ocean liner's opulent first-class dining room at six in the evening, two hours
before the appointed dinnertime, watching a maître d' offer
our four-year old twins the grand gastronomic menu, with
a bow. The lobster bisque and the oysters did not appeal to
the girls. There were several other young children aboard,
but they were all supervised by nannies or governesses. We

were the only parents in the chandeliered dining room. "Do you have any plain macaroni and cheese?" Edith asked.

We experienced a moment of triumph when in the finals of the shipboard table tennis tournament Edith beat the bodyguard of fellow passenger Yakov Malik, the Soviet ambassador to the U.N. That same evening, the movie we were watching in the ship's luxurious cinema was interrupted by our names flashing across the screen. We had left the twins asleep in the cabin, having asked the steward to look in on them every so often. We found our children running wildly along the echoing hallways and gangways, wailing for their mommy and daddy.

Upon landing in Cherbourg, the first order of business was to park the children with my parents in Amsterdam before driving to Paris to find a home and office space. Jimmy Johnson, a partner in George Ball's law firm, who two years earlier had spoken to Hill about "that young man in New York who has ideas about international public relations," invited us to have dinner at his home. It so happened that he was returning to the firm's headquarters in New York shortly. His house, in the commune of Saint-Cloud, across the river from the center of Paris, was up for rent. It was half of a gorgeous home, a mansion really, situated in an exclusive walled enclave inside a park.

It was just before Christmas when we saw the house in Parc de Montretout for the first time. It was all lit up; it radiated warmth and comfort. Jimmy and his wife said they'd had a wonderful time living there. Did we want to take it over? There was plenty of room for me to conduct business from home—a way to economize. We came back the next day to look it over, and, seduced by the romance of the place, signed the lease with the owners on the spot. All that remained was to return to Amsterdam to pick up our little girls.

We arrived in Paris in January of 1955 in a driving, wintry rain: two unhappy four-year-olds in the back of our Ford Fairlane, and Edith, my co-pilot, inventor of fairy tales, distributor of snacks and decoder of the city's street map, beside me in the passenger seat. We were all tired from the long drive as we crossed the bridge across the Seine that would bring us to our new home in Saint-Cloud. Our American car had come over in the hold of the *Queen Elizabeth* at company expense—a perk bestowed on us by corporate largesse.

The Ford Fairlane was by far our most valuable possession. The 1955 Ford model was a big white American monster with showy chrome fins, and it was far too wide for France's narrow streets. We soon realized that we were a curiosity. Our car was probably the first of its kind that the French in their cramped little 2CVs had ever seen. It notably drew the attention of the *gendarmes*; we were frequently stopped. Where was our license plate? they wanted to know. We had to explain that where we came from, cars only had one license plate. Our car didn't have a front plate. The police were always studiously polite, but we definitely roused their curiosity, if not some mild envy; they would scrutinize our driver licenses and passports at length before finally waving us on with a magnanimous *"Bon, allez-y…"*

Like our car, our home turned out to be a bit over the top. We had never lived in such palatial quarters, and it took a while to adapt to all that grand space. The Johnsons and their children had lived there with two maids and a driver. For us the reality was different; we could not afford so much help. Only Blanchette, the live-in maid, stayed. She became our savior, our lifeline, and our trusted guide to the intricacies of running a French household. Blanchette's fiancé, a municipal fireman in uniform, immediately took it upon himself to instruct us on the other aspects of life in Saint-Cloud; specifically, how to evacuate if the house ever caught fire.

The house was located inside a gated community of imposing villas in the Parc de Montretout, at one time the grounds of the Château de Saint-Cloud. The chateau itself, once occupied by the likes of Marie Antoinette and the Bonapartes, had been destroyed in the Franco-Prussian war, but the magnificent park remains to this day. One of the bonuses of the house was that it came with a key to a private gate into the park, with its wide paths, horse trails, and splendid views of the Seine and Paris in the distance. We imagined our girls running around to their hearts' content. In reality, there was no playground or any other indication that young children were tolerated; straying off the neatly raked paths was strictly forbidden.

Entering the gate into the front yard of our house, one was greeted by a bust of Victor Hugo, who, we were told, had been a friend of our landlord's father. Monsieur and Madame Capron, the owners, lived in the other, smaller half of the villa. Mr. Capron was a painter; his wife, Marcelle, was the theater critic for *Combat*, a Paris rag that had started life during the War as a broadsheet of the Resistance movement, with Camus as editor and Sartre and Malraux among its other illustrious contributors. They were a charming older couple, but kept to themselves. They weren't alone in this: we soon found out that the French in general were in the habit of jealously guarding their privacy.

The house had two kitchens, three sets of stairs, and ample, grandly furnished rooms entered through heavy double doors. Our lofty living room had a spiral staircase leading to a balcony wide enough to accommodate a chamber music ensemble, lined with floor-to-ceiling bookcases. A huge Venetian chandelier hung over the dining room table that could seat up to eighteen people. The interiors had been used for the 1949 film *Le Silence de la Mer* (Silence of the Sea) by the filmmaker Jean-Pierre Melville, a disturbing resistance story based on the novel by Vercors.

Like most old houses, ours had its drawbacks. It was cold and drafty; the bathrooms were primitive by American standards, as was the electric system. One dark wintry day, the lights in the kitchen went out. First Mr. Capron tried tackling the problem himself, diving into a tall closet housing a great many fuses. After several hours he was joined by an elderly electrician. The two old gentlemen, armed with two antique lanterns, spent a long time in the stuffy, smelly closet, arguing and disentangling wires. As evening fell, the electrician announced that he was going home for his dinner; he would return and stay all night if need be. It was at that moment that four-year-old Hester pulled on my sleeve and pointed to a switch on the outside of the electric closet that was too high for her to reach. I brushed her off, but she persisted, so that I felt obliged to tell the electrician. Ignoring me at first, he was finally persuaded to stomp over to the spot Hester had indicated. He pressed the button, and the lights came on.

The back garden was separated from the neighbors by high walls on both sides. Early on, our twins, playing on the balcony, grew excited when they spotted two little girls who had managed to climb the wall from the other side. The girls' pleas—couldn't they come over and play?—fell on deaf ears. Soon an adult appeared and barked at the girls to climb down and return inside. We decided to send the twins to the village nursery school, hoping they would make friends there. But there was no play and no interaction with the other children. The strict teacher made the children sit still at their desks the entire morning; she wouldn't even let them go to the bathroom. So in March we enrolled them in the English-speaking UNESCO nursery school, which was much more like the one they had attended in New York. It wasn't exactly next door, but Edith was able to join a carpool with other expat families living close by. An added bonus was that on playdates the children could sometimes have the American food they craved, such as Graham crackers and pasteurized milk, which the American families could obtain through the PX.

Although the twins didn't like the unfamiliar French food—they hated the pungent taste of unpasteurized milk—, for Edith and me, the cuisine was a revelation. Blanchette may have been an average French cook, but to us her dishes were simply heaven. Blanchette's Vichyssoise was more delicious than any I have had since in the best restaurants in the world. Food shopping in the village, however, was challenging. Blanchette and her fiancé were fond of eating the reasonably-priced horsemeat; she was unable to persuade our family to try it. Like every other French housewife, Edith had to shop for groceries almost every day, since there was little or no refrigeration. For the first month or two, the village butcher kept pressing his choicest cuts on her. They were also his most expensive. When Edith finally asked him to suggest something more modestly priced, he was astonished. But you Americans, you only like *ze big entrecôte*, the butcher objected. When Edith said she was in fact from *Hollande*, he walked out from behind his counter to shake her hand, saying he knew the *Hollandais* had suffered during the war almost as much as the French. From that day on, the butcher was her friend, and revealed to her the secrets of the more economical cuts.

In the late spring we were finally invited to have tea with the Caprons. Thus far we had mainly been aware of their presence through the smell of their cooking, since our kitchens were located back to back. Tea was a rather stiff occasion. To break the ice I said how nice it was to wake up every morning to a lovely view: Monsieur Capron had painted a large pastel mural of Venice's Piazza San Marco on the wall facing the bed in our master bedroom. Edith felt the need to apologize for the racket our children sometimes made running up and down the echoing parquet floors. The Caprons were gracious, but stonily reserved. They had two granddaughters a few years older than our twins, who were eager to play with Marianne and Hester when visiting. The twins were invited over to tea several times; Edith, who would have given anything for some company, was not.

One fine day Monsieur Capron announced that he would paint a portrait of the twins. We eagerly assented, not thinking of how difficult it would be to get the girls to stay still for hours at a time. Sitting side by side in a big leather arm-chair, Marianne and Hester were a pitiful sight, squirm-ing, twisting, trying to suck their thumbs. Even bribes had limited success in getting them to pose quietly. Monsieur Capron was not amused. How could he paint, he tut-tutted, under such circumstances? The portrait, as far as we knew, was never completed.

From our hill a steep stone staircase led down into the center of Saint-Cloud. It was a handy shortcut, but not very practical if you had to climb back up with a heavy shopping basket or tired toddlers. I always took the train into Paris; Edith used the Ford for driving the children to school, shopping and visiting friends. We were a typical bourgeois family. Except that wherever we went, our white Ford stamped us as unmistakably American.

When I came home one evening, Edith greeted me excitedly: she was finally starting to feel confident about her French. She told me she had taken the car into Saint-Cloud that morning. Driving down a narrow, one-way cobbled street, she had come upon a roadblock: a truck parked carelessly in the middle of the street, outside a bar. The driver was enjoying his mid-morning *petit verre de blanc* inside. There was just enough room for a Citroën or Renault to pass, but not the Ford Fairlane. After sitting there for a few minutes, repeatedly honking her horn, Edith noticed two grinning faces in the window. The truck driver and his mate seemed to be having a good laugh at her expense. Furious, she got out of the car, marched into the bar and snapped at the driver in impeccable French, *"Vous n'êtes pas un gentilhomme et maintenant foutez-moi le camp!*" ("You are no gentleman and now f... the hell off!") The driver left without finishing his wine and drove off. Edith was so elated at having mastered the proper *argot* that she felt she could face any Frenchman from now on.

Paris in 1955 was not a very welcoming city. It was cold-hearted and gloomy. France was still suffering from the wounds inflicted during World War II, its citizens trying to cope with the war's unresolved moral ambiguities. The war was still the subject of many a conversation. As newcomers and outsiders, we tried to be neutral listeners, nodding sympathetically when the complex questions the French were grappling with came up: why some folks had only stopped collaborating with the Germans near the end of the war, for example, or why so few of them had done anything about the persecution of the Jews. The Dutch were facing similar questions, but in France the answers were more opaque, and created a tangibly nervous atmosphere. War-weary France was suffering a national hangover.

I was finding, however, that the Parisians were united on one issue: they did not like upstart America. It was now nine years since VE Day, almost a decade since the Marshall Plan had started pulling the country out of its economic and financial slump. Yet France was a morass of distrust, pitting self-conscious Gaullists against nervous supporters of the disgraced Vichy regime (many of whom denied they'd had anything to do with it), as well as a powerful bloc in the middle that had sat on its hands during the Nazi occupation. To make matters worse, the effort to re-impose colonial authority in Indochina was not going well. The French Army's recent defeat at Dien Bien Phu at the hands of the North Vietnamese guerillas had caused national shock waves. To the realists, it was clear that Indochina would inevitably be lost. But millions of Frenchmen retained an unshakable faith in their army and the redoubtable Foreign Legion. I did meet some Frenchmen who, loud in their loathing of all things American, nevertheless seemed to be quietly praying that the French Army would manage to hang in there until the U.S. decided to step in.

A series of weak coalition governments also had to contend with the problem of Algeria. In November 1954, one month before our arrival, the FLN rebels had launched the first well-planned assault against the French colonial settlers. It would take another eight years and one million lives for Algeria to gain its independence.

I remember having lunch one day with Jean Choppin de Janvry, an aristocratic gentleman who ran the public relations department of Esso (later Exxon) in France. De Janvry did not have much good to say about the state of our profession in France, but did make the gloomy prediction that in about fifty years, France would be in big trouble because of its open-door policy to immigrants from Algeria, Morocco and the other African colonies.

It was an inauspicious time to be stranded alone, with no clear instructions, and no back-up plan, in a capital inhospitable to U.S. interests. No plan whatsoever had been drawn up for my transfer to Europe. John Hill had simply declared that I would start from scratch, just as he himself had done in Cleveland, Ohio, back in 1927. I had not had the gumption to point out that there was a big difference. Hill had started out with two clients; I had none. Hill knew his territory — the city of Cleveland and the steel industry. By contrast, I drew a complete blank on all fronts. My boss was giving me a chance: I would be Hill & Knowlton's man in Europe. The other members of the H&K management team, Bert Goss and Dick Darrow, did not share Hill's faith in me. I had heard that back in New York, they called me "Hill's Folly". I had no client, no plan, no company bank account, no office, no secretary, no support. I arrived with a Dutch passport, a company car, and an American green card. The details we had not discussed beforehand included my legal status in France, whether I needed a work permit, and whether I should set up a *Société à Responsabilité Limi-tée* (Limited Liability Company). I had given no thought to any of this; neither, it seemed, had my boss. I was enthusiastic: I was being given an opportunity. I wanted to succeed. I was prepared to wing it.

Getting installed in our new home and making the rounds of some of Hill's early contacts took roughly the first two months. At the *"Patronat"* (the French employers' association) I finally encountered the first Frenchman who was familiar with the words "Public Relations Agency." He steered me to a man named Franck Bauer who was in the same line of business as us. After a wartime stint in London as an announcer for *France Libre* at the BBC, Bauer had held several government posts, including Secretary-General of the *Comédie Française*, France's national theater. He had left to set up his own PR agency, the first of its kind in France. Rather than starting from scratch, here was an opportunity to be associated with a local firm. Bauer indicated he would be happy to do business with H&K. I met with

Franck several times. At first our discussions were inconclusive; but after receiving the blessing of my New York bosses, Franck and I agreed that his firm would represent H&K in France. That, at least, was a start.

I was working out of our home, typing up reports of my activities to send back to Hill in New York. Edith helped out where she could with secretarial duties, including sending out notices to our American clients' subsidiaries announcing that Hill & Knowlton now had a representative on the ground in the heart of Europe. I started making the same rounds John Hill had made two years earlier. I also visited our firm's contacts in the French steel industry. After brief scouting trips to London, Brussels and The Hague, where we had already located some struggling young public relations practitioners, I eventually expanded my itinerary to the other Western European capitals and major business centers where our U.S. clients were operating: Zurich, Geneva, Hamburg, Frankfurt, Milan, Rome, Stockholm and Madrid. I also made the rounds of the U.S. embassies and consulates, American law firms, banks and their foreign affiliates, as well as some of the large American-owned advertising agencies. I developed a standard line of inquiry: were there any local PR firms that could serve the needs of Hill & Knowlton's clients? Often the people I approached were puzzled by the question. I had to explain over and over again that I didn't mean publicity or promotion. Public Relations was an entirely new concept to many of the local managers, something they had never heard of or thought about.

I was constantly on the road or in the air. It sometimes felt as if I were searching for the proverbial needle in the haystack.

PR consultancies were few and far between. By and large, their existence hung by a thread; they were almost all in the embryonic stage. Just a very few journalists or ex-corporate PR executives had taken the plunge so far and set themselves up as independent consultants. Great Britain was the most advanced in this area: there were more PR agencies and PR departments in London than in all the countries of the Continent combined. Some of these PR men—there were no women to speak of yet—were employed by multinational corporations, many of them American-owned.

In London two years earlier, Hill had had talks with Alan Campbell-Johnson. Alan's firm represented a number of well-known American companies in the UK. He had been press attaché to Lord Mountbatten, the last Viceroy of India, and had witnessed the subcontinent's bloody partition into the two adversarial states of India and Pakistan. Upon returning to London to start his agency, Campbell-Johnson became known for using his high-society connections to bring in business. He was just the sort of partner Hill was looking for: a seasoned professional with impressive contacts and an excellent reputation. All that was left for me was to seal the deal.

Once Edith and I were settled, we were keen to open our home to our friends; there was plenty of room for guests, and visitors were a welcome distraction for Edith and the children. My parents came for an extended stay, as did other friends from Holland. One of these was a survivor of Bergen Belsen who had been Edith's pediatrician before the war. When we saw him on a visit to Amsterdam, we felt sorry for him: it was clear he could use a break. We invited him to come and stay, and he immediately accepted, saying that the waters at Enghien-les-Bains, north of Paris, would do him good. It wasn't long before we started regretting the invitation, however. He would leave for the spa very early every morning, and when he returned in the afternoon expected to be served a hot lunch after the rest of the family had already finished theirs. He acted as if our house was a hotel, was critical of the way we dealt with our children and showed himself to be less than fond of the species. He smoked my cigarettes and criticized my wine, offering nothing, not even a token treat for the kids, in return. Cowed by the concentration camp tattoo on his forearm, we dared not complain. But after two weeks, and no indication he was ever planning to leave, we finally decided his time was up. I got up at the crack of dawn to make sure I caught him to deliver the message before he left for the spa.

On another occasion, we had the bright idea of taking a visiting Dutch couple to the theater. A famous acting troupe from Holland was taking part in the International Sarah Bernhardt Festival, performing *Oedipus Rex* in our own native tongue. It was a depressing experience. The hall was nearly deserted; the Dutch interpretation rang hollow. Two ladies sitting in the row in front of us remarked loudly that they loved Dutch people but had never realized how much the language resembled a throat disease. Perhaps a more rewarding night out was when we went to hear the stunning *chanteuse* Juliette Gréco in a cabaret on the Left Bank. Like Edith Piaf, whom we had seen at the Olympia theater on our Paris honeymoon, Gréco exemplified the prevailing melancholic mood in France.

Our social life revolved largely around the American expatriate community. Our closest friends were Lou Bley, the European correspondent of New York's *Journal of Commerce*, and his wife Nellie, a born *Parisienne*, who took it upon herself to instruct and advise Edith in all matters French: fashion, recipes, decoration, coiffure, bargains and gossip. One day I came home to find my wife sitting on the couch with a striking new look; I hardly recognized her. She had been persuaded by the hairdresser to have a *coup de soleil*, a very expensive streaked hairdo. She didn't know whether to laugh or cry. Neither did I.

On one of the rare evenings we were invited to dinner in a Parisian home, our host, a business contact, was bent on showing off how the French entertain. His debonair wit was hard for us to follow, however, because of his heavy Provençal accent. When the dessert was served, he announced he had a surprise for us. A large platter was brought to the table with a lumpy object covered by a napkin. When he had the attention of all the guests, he whipped off the napkin with a flourish, revealing, to gasps of admiration, amusement, and embarrassment, a marble sculpture of an entwined Lesbian couple.

Paris wasn't called the City of Love for nothing, as Edith was to find out. She was still working on her Masters degree in psychology; her professors at Amsterdam University were letting her pursue her studies from afar. One lunchtime, after dropping the twins off at the home of a little playmate so that she could study, she walked along the wide boulevard flanking the right bank of the Seine with her textbook under her arm. Suddenly a succession of cars started pulling up beside her, gesturing at her to get in. It dawned on her that she was being propositioned. One of the drivers shouted that he wished to negotiate a price. Edith held up the heavy tome she was carrying, with the title *Psychology* printed in bold green letters, for the would-be johns to read. This did not deter them, however; they kept pestering her. Finally she ducked into a café, and telephoned me to come rescue her. Our friends later explained that Frenchmen liked to enjoy a quickie on their lunch break. All the working girls must have been already taken that day—or out to lunch.

In the 1950s Paris had rediscovered its style, if it had ever lost it; for even during the German occupation, many of the fashion houses had happily supplied their wares to the wives and girlfriends of the Nazi dignitaries and the many Frenchwomen whose men were profiting from the new regime. The post-war couture business too was booming, and visiting American clients who brought their wives over with them would ask me to obtain tickets to fashion shows—Lanvin, Molyneux, Chanel and Christian Dior, inventor of the "New Look". I tried to oblige, but it was a task I had little expertise in, or appetite for.

One of our oil company clients was setting up a public relations department at its subsidiary in England. The clueless young man appointed to be the PR manager was sent to visit me in Paris to learn what public relations was all about. He was scheduled to stay three full days, and we talked in our living room. He would roll in apologetically rather late in the day, explaining that he had been up all night, at the Crazy Horse Saloon or some other Parisian strip joint. It was obvious that this straight-laced, tweed-jacketed Englishman was more interested in his nighttime endeavors than in learning the ins and outs of our profession; in any case, I'd exhausted my font of advice and expertise the first day. When he finally came to say goodbye, he seemed rather distracted. I suspected it was because he was nervous about what to tell his bosses, and what to hide from his wife.

In the spring, John Hill made a special trip to Paris to attend a royal event organized by Ed Barrett, whose public affairs outfit H&K had recently acquired.[8] Barrett, a former Public Information officer at the U.S. State Department, was retained by the Duke and Duchess of Windsor to do damage control. Since abdicating from the British throne to marry the divorcée Mrs. Wallis Simpson, the Duke had seen his popularity take a nosedive. The pair liked Ed's plan to boost their image: they would sponsor an annual award in Paris for the most promising up-and-coming artist.

The award that year went to the avant-garde artist Jean Dubuffet. At the reception in the Hotel George V, I shook hands with the royal couple and stood next to John Hill as he engaged in a painfully stiff and vacuous conversation with them. The dangerously elegant Mrs. Simpson spoke the few words that were exchanged. The Prince stayed in the background and never opened his mouth. I doubted that any of them had any interest in modern art; John Hill certainly didn't.

I had high hopes as I accompanied Hill to a lunch at Lasserre, to which we were invited by a group of European

---

8 Ed Barrett later left H&K to become Dean of Columbia University's School of Journalism, where he founded the Columbia Journalism Review.

steel company executives. It was the most exquisite meal I had ever had, but nothing came of it. Our hosts' hospitality turned out to be just a polite gesture of friendship toward Mr. Hill as the representative of their colleagues in the States. They had no interest in exploring the possibility of PR representation; Europe didn't need it, they said. After the lunch, I walked Hill back to his hotel and confessed my frustration and doubts. Maybe the naysayers were right, I said; maybe it was indeed a folly to expect this to work. To my surprise, Hill told me not to give up. He was convinced the tide would turn, and he wanted his firm to be ahead of the pack when it did.

At home, long waits by the telephone for international connections were part of my daily routine. In the intervals between business trips, I did a lot of pacing up and down in our elegant living room with the spiral staircase and book gallery above. In those days, and for many decades thereafter, Hill & Knowlton did not overtly solicit new business. John Hill's credo was that we were never to chase after clients. We should simply position ourselves in such a way that a potential client would run into us, and perhaps decide it could use our help. Since I couldn't actively drum up business, actual billable work was unpredictable and all too sporadic. Sometimes I had to hold my breath and bite my tongue for as long as six weeks before an overture led to something concrete. "If these last eight months have taught me one thing," I wrote in a letter to John in the fall, "it is that the public relations practitioner in Europe is a rather frustrated creature."

It was a difficult and disappointing uphill struggle. I had no clients to speak of, no colleagues or staff to exchange views or gossip with. One bright spot was meeting Procter & Gamble's man in Europe. P & G was a major U.S. client of ours. Tom Bower had been sent to Paris to explore and build up Procter's business on the Continent, after a stint the company's only wholly-owned European manufacturing plant in Newcastle, England. He and I got on well together. We shared similar working conditions; he too was on his own, working out of his home. Procter & Gamble soon took off as an unstoppable global marketing force. My acquaintanceship with Tom would pay off when a booming P&G eventually became a powerful presence in Europe.

I began to question whether Paris was the right place to be stationed. Saint-Cloud was quite a haul from both Le Bourget and Orly, the two airports I most frequently flew out of. And the problem of finding inexpensive office space remained unsolved. One evening, returning late from the airport after yet another unproductive week, I found my wife and children fast asleep. Looking at those innocent faces, I felt a chill. I suddenly saw myself back in the prison camp in the jungle: the beatings, the starvation, the deaths. Was what I was doing now *real*? Was I really here, living in one of the great capitals of the world, in peace time, with a lovely wife and two children, healthy, clothed, well-fed and learning to appreciate a good glass of Burgundy? Couldn't it all vanish in an instant? What about my futile search for clients? John Hill's patience, my wife's belief in me, and my own confidence that I would somehow make it—was any of it justified?

I was ambitious and naïve at the same time. I knew that some American corporations in Europe were doing a fine job of adapting to local mores. But others—and they were many—were quite strikingly failing to adapt their aims and business practices to the countries in which they were operating. Those companies were living up to the epithet of "the ugly American," by sending over managers who did not speak the language, and were insufficiently sensitive to their host countries' customs and conventions. All of them, it seemed to me, could be doing a better job. If only they would ask me!

One area where I did make some headway was in signing up associates. Besides the ones already mentioned—Alan Campbell-Johnson in London and Franck Bauer in Paris—I found compatible partners in Belgium and the Netherlands, and worked out a retainer arrangement with them. Eric Cyprès, in Brussels, was selling advertising for the *New York Herald Tribune* when we met; his partner had been the Belgian prime minister's press attaché. In The Hague I found Frans Hollander, who had held similar information posts in the Dutch government. The problem was that in many other European countries, Germany for instance, the self-important but relatively inexperienced corporate counselors I encountered had not yet gained any traction. In Italy there were no independent PR agencies at all. The virgin field was wide open.

Finally, at the end of the year, came the breakthrough I had been praying for. We won the Brussels World's Fair account. Thanks to Eric Cyprès, the Belgian government made Hill & Knowlton PR counsel to its World's Fair, to be held in 1958. Our brief covered activities in the U.S., the U.K., France, Germany, Belgium and Holland. I was appointed coordinator of the account. I couldn't wait to get started.

Meanwhile Edith was not having an easy time of it in Paris. With her husband away so much of the time, and lacking family or close friends, it was a lonely existence. She had recently taken up pottery, taking lessons from a potter whose studio was located in the gatehouse of our compound; but she was feeling increasingly isolated, missing both Amsterdam and New York. She cheered up when she found herself pregnant again. We were both delighted and decided it would be best if the baby was born in Amsterdam, in familiar surroundings among family and friends, and in the care of our old family doctor, who five years earlier had entertained me (and exhausted Edith) in the delivery room with an endless repertoire of Jewish jokes.

New York management agreed that it did not matter where in Europe I lived. At the end of 1955 we moved back to the Netherlands, just in time for baby Jessica's birth.

5

////////////////////////////////

HOLLAND ON THE REBOUND

We had less than three months until the baby was born, and so were in a hurry to find a place to live. My immediate focus was to put a roof over my family's head. Although we had left Holland only five years earlier, we felt like aliens again, only now it was in our own native country. Moving back to Amsterdam felt no different than our move to Baltimore, or Paris; it was difficult, there were new conditions to be adapted to all over again. I berated myself: was I dragging my family into a life of continuous migrations?

The Netherlands was in the throes of a severe housing crisis. Ten years after the war, the country was still licking its wounds. Although it had availed itself of America's generous Marshall Plan aid, this had only taken the edge off the pains of a stuttering economy. The loss of the East Indies with its valuable raw materials had dealt a serious blow to Holland's wealth. The country was still not in an especially comfortable or hopeful place. When we visited relatives and old friends, the conversation still seemed to revolve around the same old subjects— the war, the Germans, who was in the Resistance and who had been a collaborator. Their universe had remained narrow, while we, world travelers now, had gained a wider perspective; we were ready for something new.

The national housing shortage became our main preoccupation. There were no unfurnished rentals to be had. As newcomers, our names were at the very bottom of lengthy waiting lists for rent-controlled apartments. The few available houses or apartments for sale in Amsterdam or The Hague were out of our price range. In the unregulated real estate market, prices had soared out of sight.

Our search for shelter became an all-absorbing activity. We explored every lead in Holland's limited real estate inventory. Finally recognizing that to find a place we liked would take months, if not years, we took out a lease on one furnished rental, then another. Each had more drawbacks than comfort and amenities. A landlady's cat took out its ire on us by leaving excrement between our sheets. The smell of boiled cabbage and potatoes was an unpleasant reminder of wartime deprivation. Compared to our antiquated but spacious accommodations in Parc de Montretout, Amsterdam's housing felt dull, drab, cramped and uninspiring.

We were still living in a furnished flat in Amsterdam when Edith went into labor. I had just flown back from Bremen; upon disembarking I was greeted with the news that my wife had been taken to the hospital. A car was parked on the tarmac next to the plane to whisk me through the airport without passing through customs and immigration. I made it to the hospital just in time for baby Jessica's arrival.

A few months later we finally moved into a brand-new row house in Zandvoort, the seaside resort half an hour's drive from Amsterdam. The modest house, part of a new development, was reasonably priced; it had a small front yard and a pleasant back garden. Our street was situated on the edge of the dunes, a stone's throw from the splendid white-sand beaches of the North Sea. Our firm's associate in the Netherlands, the appropriately named Frans Hollander, had offered me space in his offices in The Hague. By American standards, the commute from Zandvoort to The Hague, a forty-five minute drive, was not arduous, but to my parents and our friends our choice of Zandvoort seemed a curious decision.

Our two years in Zandvoort were peaceful and happy. There were plenty of children for the girls to play with, and our own social life was much improved. One evening we decided to bring a dash of cosmopolitan flair to our village by turning the top floor of our house into a French bistro for a wine and cheese soirée. The party was a big success, with its red-checkered tablecloths and exotic stinky cheeses, a new taste to most of the guests. My wife was an expert at devising ways to make parties fun: on another occasion, all the men were given the task of fashioning a hat for their spouses from a miscellany of odd bits and pieces before dinner. We became such good friends with the local pediatrician, Elly Den Hartog, and her husband Joel, that our two families took a winter vacation together in Switzerland's Bernese Oberland. Elly, a very smart woman, sported an Auschwitz tattoo on her arm, but never brought up the subject. She treated the numbers on her arm, a monstrosity branded into her in a concentration camp, with complete outward indifference. By contrast, my parents' upstairs neighbor, who also tended to wear sleeveless dresses to show off her tattoo, let you know it was "for the whole world to see what the Germans did." Hardly a day passed without a headline referring back to the war. The wounds healed slowly.

One day we hatched a plot with Elly and Joel to play a practical joke on some of our friends. I don't know what possessed us, but we all thought it would be a lark. The wives had been discussing how impossible it was to get help. It was decided that Edith and I would throw a dinner party, and Elly and Joel would pretend to be the maid and butler. We would play the same role for them at a future date, and whichever couple received the biggest tip would be the winner. The guests were people who did not know the Den Hartogs. The dinner went off without a hitch; Elly and Joel, in rented costumes, played their subservient, invisible roles to perfection. At the end of the meal, Joel came in, bowed, and whispered in my ear that they were done, and would be going. A few minutes later the front doorbell rang, and there stood Elly and Joel, having changed into evening clothes, saying they were sorry to have missed the dinner. "Come in for a nightcap anyway," we gushed. The upshot was that none of the other guests recognized them as the couple who had just served the dinner, and we, suddenly embarrassed by our stunt, did not have the guts to reveal the deception. Edith finally blurted out, "But don't you recognize them?" To which one of the guests replied vaguely, "Yes, perhaps, haven't we met before?" We never had a chance to reciprocate the joke, to my great relief.

In my professional life I was still having a hard time gaining recognition; the need for public relations was a hard concept for Europeans to grasp. One day I received a call from a small local glass manufacturer, who wanted to get some publicity for his firm in neighboring Belgium. I referred the business to our Brussels associate, Eric Cyprès. Some months later, the client refused to pay Eric's bill. We decided to handle the matter ourselves in small claims court. I presented what I thought was a rational case for our billing system, based on time spent. Like most of his compatriots, the civil judge had never before heard of public relations, and could not fathom what the invoice was for. He threw out our case with a shrug.

We stayed in Holland for four years, from early 1956 to the end of 1959. During that period I must have spent more than a third of my waking hours in airports, on planes and on long drives to the neighboring countries. At night I would eat a lonely meal in the hotel restaurant. But it paid off in the end; I did eventually succeed in building a small but cohesive international organization. This was in no little part thanks to our involvement in the 1958 Brussels World's Fair.

It had all started in New York. In 1954 the Belgian government had approached Hill & Knowlton because of a specific American problem. It was the height of the Cold War. As plans for the Brussels Fair, the first World's Fair since the one held in New York in 1939, began to take shape, the Soviet Union announced it would build a massive pavilion that would dominate one whole side of the Fairgrounds, with the intention of scoring a significant propaganda victory. Lawmakers in Washington felt it was important to steal some of the Communists' thunder by building an equally dazzling showcase promoting not only the United States' cultural and scientific achievements, but its prosperous capitalist lifestyle as well. The problem was that neither the State Department nor any other government agency had the power to fund a project four years into the future. The necessary congressional appropriation would only be considered one year before the Fair opened, which left too little time to complete such an undertaking. Please fix this Washington problem for us, the Belgians requested. We were, of course, happy to oblige. The money was appropriated in time, and the splendid U.S. pavilion was built right next door to the Soviet exhibit—an example, some said, of the Belgians' sense of humor.

I was summoned to New York to be introduced to this important new client. John Hill and his wife Elena were hosting a cocktail party at their New York apartment. The party was in full swing when I arrived. Standing at the bar, I introduced myself to a pleasant-looking, rather rotund gentleman. *"Enchanté,"* he said; "it appears that I am the guest of honor." This was Count Moens de Fernig, the Belgian High Commissioner of the World's Fair. He said that he would need help in bringing Expo-58, as it was called, to the attention of not only American visitors, but also attendees from Europe, well ahead of the inauguration. "Well then, you've come to the right place," I said. "We have a public relations team in place in France, Germany, the Netherlands and England, and can provide you with plenty of ideas for drumming up interest." The Fair, I suggested, would help

Europe to turn its back on the past; it was just what was needed to energize the public. Well into the noisy evening, we were suddenly plunged into darkness: a New York City blackout. Elena Hill, in true PR fashion, came up with a quick solution. She and her helpers sailed into the room with several large candelabras, and the party continued by candlelight, as if Elena had planned it that way.

Nearly 15,000 workers spent three years building the 500-acre World's Fair site outside Brussels. Its centerpiece was the giant Atomium, a massive aluminum-clad construction of nine interconnected spheres symbolizing the peaceful use of atomic energy. The structure still attracts visitors to this day. For the next two years I spent at least two or three days every month in Brussels. Our work consisted mainly of preparing campaigns to attract the hordes of visitors required to make the Expo a success. To do this, we had to draw the interest of government officials and politicians, travel agents, educators, and media of all stripes. Our team was frequently called to Brussels for progress reports and strategy sessions. It was the first major test to see how our various associates worked as a team. I was the coordinator of client activities. Our first meeting got off to a less than auspicious start: Alan Campbell-Johnson had left his passport at home in London. Luckily a phone call to the High Commissioner was all it took to get him past the immigration officials at Brussels Airport.

Of our entire international team, Alan Campbell-Johnson was by far the most articulate, though long-winded, spokesman. His ease with some of the aristocratic officials we had to deal with was most useful. I often visited him in his London flat, located within the range of the bells of Westminster that summoned Members of Parliament back to the Chamber when it was time for a vote. It was a gathering place for British Liberals, a party that in the 1950s was very much in the minority. During one of the soirees I attended there, I met Jo Grimond, the party leader, a tall man with sensible ideas.

I once happened to mention to Alan that although I loved the view of the Thames from my room in the Savoy, I found the hotel charges exorbitant. On my next visit Alan arranged for me to stay at the Liberal Club, located next door to the Savoy, with an equally attractive view of the river, at the ridiculously modest price of fifteen shillings per night. Alan's office was just off Piccadilly; he usually took me to lunch at the St. James's Club, a favorite haunt of British diplomats. The entry hall featured a marble staircase leading up to the dining room. Every time I went I was met with the sight of a bald, round-faced old gentleman sitting at the foot of the imposing stairs, as if sculpted into it. When it finally occurred to me to ask Alan about him, he introduced us: it was Calouste Gulbenkian, the oil tycoon and art collector known as "Mr. Five Per Cent" because of his habit of retaining a five per cent share in the oil companies he developed.

The few-and-far-between public relations practitioners spread out across Europe had by now found one another, and in 1955 formally established the International Public Relations Association. When I joined in 1956, I was the only consultant in the employ of a large PR firm; most of the other members were corporate in-house counselors.

Occasionally a handful of us would get together to exchange information and to have a good time. I found myself among a motley crew of rugged individualists. After all, who in his right mind entered a field that no one had ever heard of? There was Tim Traverse-Healy, for instance, a boisterous Englishman who spent his weekends driving around in his fire engine, with his half-dozen or so offspring on board. There was Lucien, a published French poet; we could not decide whether he was the best poet among PR men, or the best PR man among poets. Guido was an Italian with an impossibly long name, and Claude was the scion of a French provincial department store family. The World's Fair, it was decided, would be a good place to promote our profession, and so the first World Congress of Public Relations was held in Brussels in 1958, chaired by our very own Eric Cyprès. I was amazed at the numbers that showed up: two hundred and fifty practitioners took part, hailing from twenty-three different nations.

The World's Fair itself, opened by King Baudouin of Belgium to great fanfare on April 17, 1958, was a rousing success. Over fifty nations took part, and thanks in part to our efforts, over forty million visitors descended on Brussels to learn what the future might hold for a new and peaceful world.

6

//

THE GERMAN CONUNDRUM

In West Germany, the concept of industrial or financial public relations developed at a much slower pace than in other European countries. As I found out early on in my attempts to gain a foothold in Germany, Joseph Goebbels had been a master of political propaganda for the Hitler regime; that unwelcome association made the post-WWII German enterprises shy away from any public exposure or transparency. A luncheon in Düsseldorf with three bankers hammered home for me the German penchant for *Geheimnis*—fondness for secrecy and abhorrence of transparency. Rarely had I encountered such aversion to openness and communication. One of the bankers posed the very valid question that I would hear repeatedly throughout my career: What good is communication if we have no crisis? Some of the big companies felt differently, however, and did have in-house PR departments, which I duly visited. These included Germany's "big three" chemical companies—Bayer, Hoechst and BASF—as well as

Siemens, whose PR department was headed by Dr. Albert Oeckl, now a revered pioneer in the field.

I found that in Germany an astonishing number of professionals chose to be addressed as *Herr Doktor*, if not *Herr Professor*. At Krupp, the steel and former armaments manufacturer, I met with Prof. Dr. Hundhausen, who bent my ear with lofty, complex theories about public influence. In the lobby of the Breidenbacher Hof, one of Düsseldorf's main hotels where I frequently stayed, a bellboy would walk around with a blackboard announcing a telephone call for *"Herr General K."*. The "General", I found out, was an enterprising American businessman from the Midwest who was trying to drum up business for his own small PR agency. He was Jewish, and used his religion as a coercive marketing tool, telling German companies he was the best man to restore their reputations in Washington. By having himself paged, he had hit upon a formula that not only gave hourly evidence of his existence, but also of his status. I found out later that during the war he had served as a brigadier-general in some dim administrative corner of the Pentagon; thus the "Herr General".

My first attempt at locating a PR representative in Germany turned up Gerta Tzschaschel, a novice lobbyist who worked out of her office in Bad Godesberg, a suburb of Bonn, the West German capital. Bonn, like the rest of Germany under Chancellor Adenauer, was rebuilding with the help of Marshall Plan funds, although it still had the look of a small provincial town. My room was in the Park Hotel, a modest villa where I had to squeeze past a grand piano to reach the reception. A much grander Park Hotel was under construction next door.

Gerta was an effective lobbyist acquainted with many German politicians. She was somewhat new to the business of PR, however, and it showed. She had an uneasy relationship with the management of the German subsidiary of Gillette, one of our major U.S. clients. In the U.S., Gillette was famous for its sponsorship of spectator sports. One of my assignments was to find a similar opportunity in Germany. All we were able to come up with was rowing—a sport that was hardly the kind of mass spectacle Gillette had in mind. The company's German headquarters were based in West Berlin. The chairman was a short, genial man with a military bearing. He too liked to be addressed as *"Herr General"*. I later learned that during World War II he had been the general in charge of razor blade production for the clean-shaven German troops. Needing someone to organize a Gilette-sponsored event taking place in Denmark, we engaged a local freelancer, unaware that the man sported a full and impressive beard. Fortunately his shagginess had no significant repercussions on our relationship with Gillette.

On one of my visits to Berlin, which was still divided into American, British, French and Soviet zones, I took a taxi on a tour of East Berlin. After passing through Checkpoint Charlie, I found myself in a totally different, gloomy world. The ugly, barracks-type buildings were somber; the people on the street did not smile. The blank-faced East Germans reminded me of my own time as a prisoner of war. I did not feel any sympathy for them. To me, these men and women deserved their fate: the curse of the Holocaust should shadow them forever.

Finally I found the man we needed: Manfred Zapp, or

perhaps he found me. Manfred's Düsseldorf office became Hill & Knowlton's first real foothold in Germany. Zapp came from a long line of industrialists. In the nineteenth century the firm Krupp und Zapp was a major industrial force. The two families' forebears had founded two dynasties that were famous in the Ruhr area and well known beyond; the Zapps as distributors of steel, and the Krupps as its manufacturers. Their empire encompassed not only some of Germany's largest steel plants but also the manufacture of heavy armaments for the German armed forces. Krupp gained universal notoriety in World War I when it produced "Big Bertha," (named after the wife of a Krupp owner), then the world's largest artillery piece.

Manfred's office served the needs of our American clients and also helped out with some publicity tasks for the World's Fair. Although Manfred was well connected among the executives of some of the major companies in his area, none were prepared to employ us, since, I was told, German public opinion was already on industry's side. When I first met Manfred, then a man in his fifties, his staff consisted of one secretary and a shifty-looking young man who was the sole other employee. Just how shifty he was we found out when he made off with the contents of the petty cash box. The police informed us that the money had been converted into a one-way ticket to Mexico.

Dinner at Zapp's home was a surprisingly congenial affair that ran against my anti-German prejudices. Manfred lived in a coach house, all that remained of a large estate once owned by his forebears. He still represented a type of ancient landed gentry. He lived surrounded by a legacy of antique porcelain, heavy old furniture, landscape paintings and silver serving dishes. Those objects, like Manfred's own manner, harked back to the nineteenth century, Bismarck and a Prussian Empire, and perhaps even earlier times. I sensed that Manfred and his friends wanted to dwell in a pleasant, pre-Hitler period of civility. Manfred told me that as a young man he had joined the German Foreign Office in Berlin and served in its press department. It had been obvious to his superiors that Manfred disapproved of Nazi policies, he said. When the Hitler acolyte von Ribbentrop took over the Foreign Office, Manfred was abruptly dismissed and conscripted into the army. Asked by a high-ranking officer whether he possessed any useful skills, Manfred mentioned his work in communications. He was promptly assigned to the infantry, he told me, and for the rest of his time in uniform ordered to haul barbed wire around.

We gingerly broached the subject of the war but were hesitant to delve too deeply into it. One day in a café on the *Königsallee*, Düsseldorf's elegant shopping boulevard, Manfred expressed horror at what his compatriots had done to the Jews. Being on German soil, I was neither prepared nor in the mood to question his sincerity. In contrast to the fury I had felt in East Berlin, my attitude toward West Germans was decidedly mellow. Was it because the people I met did not avoid speaking about the past, or was it merely that they were so friendly to me? Had I become superficial in my judgment, giving these Germans a pass? Or was I simply comparing their attitude to that of the Japanese? On my visit to Tokyo in 1953, the Japanese had stonewalled every attempt I made to find even one person who was prepared to exchange views about our wartime experiences. By contrast, the German press and many ordinary Germans, especially the younger generation, had no compunction about discussing the sins of their elders. The world at large recognized that the German government was leaning over backwards to remedy Holocaust suffering through substantial payments to the State of Israel and through a program called *Wiedergutmachung* (financial reparations) to Jewish survivors and their children. I found it hard to picture amiable Manfred as a guard in a concentration camp, or even as a hated Nazi soldier. And yet I sometimes wondered whether he was telling the truth. Then I would remind myself that as a well-connected supporter of the Adenauer regime's Christian Democrats, he must be. Chancellor Adenauer, popular in the West, was hailed as a leader intent on rebuilding a democratic and economically viable West German Republic, albeit with a large dose of American financial aid.

Manfred knew his Rhine, Saar and Moselle wines, but was also known for draining a whole bottle of *Steinhäger* schnapps every night before bed. In the morning, back at his desk, Manfred exhibited no sign of being any the worse for wear. He remained always in complete control of himself, the perfect gentleman, neatly dressed in tweedy sports jackets.

Manfred's social circle was a close group of friends who came to his home to enjoy the comfortable, old-fashioned atmosphere. They gathered around the heavy mahogany table to eat asparagus from the garden or wild boar shot by one of the guests, and drink one of Manfred's fine wines. In the largely desolate Ruhr area, few spots could have been as pleasant as Manfred's house. Conversation revolved around current bestsellers, or Düsseldorf's theater or concert offerings. They were businessmen, journalists and academics, like Professor Wolfgang Mommsen, a historian of note. Mommsen was a tall man with a broad forehead and large hands. He dominated the conversation in a soft but authoritative voice; the other guests looked up to him, especially the younger men, managers of various local enterprises. Manfred's guests displayed the deference to their seniors that I associated with Germany's culture of obedience. The wives were mere background ornaments; they did not participate in their husbands' conversation but sat quietly or spoke in soft tones about matters unrelated to the men's talk. I wondered: was this the new or a very ancient Germany?

The subject of Germany's recent past did occasionally come up, never as a main topic, but in passing. What came out then was a sort of deep communal sigh, which I took to be a sign of reluctant guilt, although I was too timid to ask. The company's lighthearted banter and the respect the younger generation showed toward Zapp and his contemporaries made me think they could not have been Nazis.

In Holland, it was a point of principle among most of the people we knew to refuse to buy a Volkswagen, a Bosch refrigerator, a Siemens appliance, or any other German brand. The wounds of the Nazi occupation and deportations were still too fresh. Yet turning one's back on products and persons of German origin did not stretch to turning away German tourists or their money. The Dutch seaside resorts were enormously popular with vacationing Germans, especially from the Ruhr area. During the summer months, Zandvoort was awash in Germans who rented houses from local homeowners more than willing to move their families into the garage and cash in. Yet these same burghers loved to tell the story about the Dutchman who, when asked for directions by a German in a Mercedes, would point him in the wrong direction. Or the other apocryphal response to a lost German: "I'll be happy to direct you, if you'll give me back my bike" (a reference to German wartime plundering).

Not having personally lived through the horrors of the Nazi regime made it easier for me to visit Germany without hatred or anxiety. There were some people I mistrusted, to be sure—the ones who emphasized their dislike of Hitler too vociferously, for example. But I did not buy into the prevailing perception that every German who had lived through the war was a hypocrite claiming *"Ich habe es nicht gewust"* ("I really did not know").

My rosy outlook changed the night I was accompanied to Düsseldorf by Edith, who had until then always stubbornly refused to set foot in Germany. I had been driving from Zandvoort to Düsseldorf at least once a month. She did not resent or object to my going there; she knew I had a job to do. Finally, worn down by my tales of a sympathetic Manfred Zapp and his crowd, Edith agreed one day to accompany me. Manfred had organized another of his small dinner parties. The usual crowd attended. Since everyone was having such a good time, the party did not want to break up; after dinner we all trooped into town to go dancing. We wound up in a small nightclub in one of the big hotels. One of the guests, a silver-haired, somewhat older gentleman, bowed and asked Edith to dance. He was a real charmer. When he asked her where her accent was from, Edith told him to guess. He thought she must be English. She admitted to being Dutch. "Oh, but I love your country so much, I spent some time there, the best years of my life!" "When was that?" Edith asked. "During the war," he said. "I just *love* Hollanders!" Edith froze in his arms. "I can assure you they don't love you back," she said, and asked to be led back to our table. We got up and left, Edith claiming a sudden headache. Manfred walked us out and told us that his guest, the president of a German aircraft manufacturing start-up, had been a Luftwaffe general during the war. Back at our hotel, Edith was livid. That arrogant smooth-talker would certainly have been involved in the May 1940 invasion and destruction of Rotterdam, and who knows what other horrors.

It was only many decades later, while doing research for this book, that I came upon a startling discovery. Dr. Manfred Zapp, I read, had been arrested in New York in 1941 "for not registering as a foreign agent". It appeared that he had been working in New York as the head of the American section of the Transocean News Service, and was accused of being a Nazi propagandist and spy. Germany had promptly responded to his arrest by apprehending several American newspapermen and consular officials in Europe. An exchange was arranged, and Zapp was deported via the detention facility on Ellis Island. Manfred never told me any of this. I don't recall that he ever mentioned that he had lived in the United States; nor that at the end of the war he was arrested in the Weimar city of Bad Berka, this time by the U.S. Army's Third Division. Now, of course, I kick myself for failing to exercise due diligence. Was I so relieved to have found a business partner in Germany that

I turned a blind eye, deliberately skipping the background check? Was I so blinded by Manfred's charm that I took him at face value when he professed to have been a hapless citizen caught up in events outside of his control?

In the 1960s Manfred Zapp retired to Sintra, in Portugal, and when we moved our office to Hamburg, I appointed Gerald Schröder to be our representative in Germany. A German-born U.S. citizen, Gerald had left his job as Assistant to the Publisher of *Business Week* to return to Germany after marrying a wealthy woman from Kiel. Later we also established a presence in Frankfurt, the country's financial center. In spite of our efforts, Frankfurt remained relatively unprofitable for years. It was kept afloat by the work we did for American companies in Germany such as Citibank and American Cyanimid.

The German recovery was certainly impressive. I traveled to Duisburg, in the heart of the Ruhr district, to evaluate the relationship of M.A.N., a manufacturer of heavy machinery, to its different constituencies. It was the first time I had experienced an organization whose workday started at 6 a.m., for both workers and management. At 8.a.m. there was a pause for a second breakfast, which for the executives meant a choice between a snifter of brandy or a nip of *schnapps*. Perhaps that was the secret of their stamina, I speculated, for the long day ahead. The German economic miracle was not only due to the Marshall plan, but also the result of hard work and long hours.

Helmuth Lutz was the principal of a Stuttgart law firm with whom we joined forces to help Continental Can, our common client, defend an anti-trust challenge in the High Court of the European Common Market. We had just opened a new Brussels office, as had Lutz's firm. Our client had put in a bid to acquire two large European metal container manufacturers, one German and one Dutch. The European authorities perceived this to be an unfair American invasion, threatening fair and honest local competition, even though Germany, the Netherlands and France each held well-guarded monopolies in their own protected backyards. An American takeover resulting in a foreign-owned multinational behemoth that would dominate the European market was not to be tolerated—a sentiment echoed in the local press. The legal battle this set off finally reached the European High Court in Luxemburg. It was the first case of its kind.

Helmuth and his legal team set policy; we were hired to interpret and translate the German legal mumbo-jumbo into understandable press releases in English, French, German and Dutch. Our client won the case. Although Helmuth and I worked well together, we kept our distance. I sensed in Helmuth a certain reluctance to engage with me, a Dutchman, on any subject that might put his fatherland on the spot.

Another German I had dealings with was Hermann Abs, the long-time chairman of Deutsche Bank. An immediately imposing figure, Abs was a man of great charm. He was probably the most distinguished and esteemed banker of Europe's post-war era. When I met him, he surprised me by speaking fluent Dutch. He told me that early in his career he had worked in Amsterdam, as well as having had several stints in London and the U.S. At the war's end he had been interned and interrogated for ninety days by Allied war crime investigators; he was released without being charged.

In spite of his prominent position at Deutsche Bank, Abs claimed he had managed to keep his distance from the Nazis, had never met Hitler or other party leaders, and had lent help to a number of Jewish colleagues. The picture remained rather murky, however, since throughout the war he had kept his seat on the boards of quite a few major German industrial companies that employed slave labor. But the business community was satisfied that since the Nazis had controlled all activities of any company engaged in the war effort, corporate boards had served as mere window dressing, and had not necessarily been informed or even been aware of what was happening on the production lines. It was only later that other facts long suppressed came to light, such as Abs's role in financing Hitler's war effort, or the allegation that he possessed stolen artworks.

I give this as just another example of how in those years it was deemed convenient to overlook certain business leaders' shady pasts, both in Germany and in Japan. It was in their approach, however, that members of the two former Axis powers differed, in my experience. In thirty years of doing business in Japan I never met a Japanese who would own up to any war involvement. The subject was simply off the table, never to be discussed, which, naturally, only made me more suspicious. The Germans of my generation, on the other hand, found a way to disarm me—and I was certainly not the only one[9]—by professing innocence or even ignorance of what had transpired during the Nazi years.

---

9 The next generation of Germans, of course, had already begun to ask questions about what their parents had done during the war.

7

//////////////////////////////////

EUROPE UNITED

In the early nineteen-fifties, the concept of a united Europe had started to take hold. The idea had taken shape in the mind of Jean Monnet during World War II. But turning the dream into reality was a slow process, starting on a modest scale. A first step was the birth of the European Coal and Steel Community, a coalition of the national coal and steel industries of France, West Germany, Italy, Belgium, Luxemburg and the Netherlands—the underpinnings of the Western European economies. As for me, I was captivated by the idea of a United Europe. I believed in the dream: a Europe without borders; the free flow of people across the Continent; a single currency; one flag and one national anthem; and, best of all, total disarmament and abolishment of war.

My championship of European integration was born of both environmental and genetic roots: among the participating countries, the Netherlands was one of the most ardent supporters of the idea. Since the late forties, Dutch public opinion had favored the concept of a united Europe that would prevent the outbreak of armed conflict on the Continent once and for all. European integration had been tried before, but always through military conquest. Leaders like Charlemagne, Napoleon, and Hitler had ultimately failed miserably to impose hegemony through violent means. This time, however, the circumstances were different. The mood was sober; people were sick of war. The time seemed to be ripe. The post-war leaders—Britain's Winston Churchill, Belgium's Paul-Henri Spaak and Italy's Alcide De Gasperi—were giants of moderation; even Konrad Adenauer, in West Germany, was showing a desire to drive his universally hated country back into a peaceful fold. Together they offered a promise of some kind of European common denominator.

Having been present in 1953 at the meeting in New York between John Hill and Jean Monnet, the French statesman behind the whole idea, I was excited when his colleague, Foreign Minister Robert Schuman, agreed to see me in his Quay d'Orsay office in the early sixties. A former prime minister, co-author with Monnet of the "Schuman Declaration", Schuman had done much of the conceptual work that had led to the formation of the European Coal and Steel Community, the initial economic alliance. Schuman greeted me from behind the widest desk I had ever seen, covered in towering piles of documents. Seated opposite him I felt very small. I asked him, rather naïvely, how important he thought American public opinion might be to the European project. Schuman replied that of course it was of overwhelming and indispensable importance. It was the diplomatic thing to say: he was well aware that, apart from a small number of Europhiles, the American public gave the matter little, if any, thought. Even so, the time was not ripe, he said, to allocate the necessary resources to launch a PR campaign. I had not expected much, but still I was disappointed.

However, it was largely thanks to Europe's integration that John Hill's gamble finally began to pay off. The European Coal and Steel Community grew into the European Common Market, easing the flow of goods and information within countries in which we already had a presence. It was a question of being in all the right places at the right time. In the 1970s, with the entry of Britain and Denmark, the Common Market became the European Economic Community (EEC), finally expanding into the 28-member European Union (EU) it is today. As U.S.-European trade and investment grew, so did Hill & Knowlton's transatlantic business. One of our roles was to update multinational clients in the States, such as American Cyanamid, Monsanto, Citibank and Alcoa, about what was going on in Brussels, and advise them on internal political squabbles that might lead to legislation affecting their business. Over thirty thousand European civil servants ultimately staffed the Brussels bureaucracy, spinning a web of regulations that in many instances had a direct impact on our clients. My semi-annual return visits to the U.S. were occasions for briefing clients in New York and the Midwest on the latest such developments.

The EU continued to play a role in my life after I retired. In the 1980s I received a call from Robert Schaetzel, a retired U.S. ambassador to the European Community, inviting me to join the board of the American Council of Jean Monnet Studies. This Washington-based organization was made up of a number of Schaetzel's former colleagues, diplomats who had at some time served in Brussels. I was the only non-diplomat on the board, and flew to Washington once every quarter to attend the meetings. Our work had only marginal impact, since its main activity was to grant stipends to American academics studying some aspect of the American-European relationship. I enjoyed being part of the group, all of whose members spoke nostalgically of encounters with Jean Monnet or Robert Schuman. It also gave me an opportunity to visit Emile Noel, then Secretary-General of the E.E.C. I continued to harp on the subject that had frustrated me for many years: why is so little being done in the U.S. to give people a better understanding of European integration? And why does the Brussels bureaucracy make so little effort to connect with American public opinion? Once a PR man, always a PR man.

What happens in Europe—politically, economically, in soccer, in tennis (whether Paris or Wimbledon); even in classical music—has remained a lifelong preoccupation of mine. I used to tell friends that I had "a foot on both con-tinents". It may have sounded presumptuous, but it is a fact that I cannot remember a single year in my adult life when, no matter where we lived, I did not visit the other continent at least once, or, more commonly, two or three times. The progress and setbacks of European integration continue to be of consuming interest to me. I took a dim view of Gen-eral de Gaulle when he vetoed the entry of Great Britain into the Common Market, first in 1963 and then in 1967. I remember watching a television interview with the General during France's 1967 election campaign, in the crowded living room of a Dutch friend. To a group of pro-Europe Dutchmen, de Gaulle came across as arrogant, autocratic and bombastic. He handily won reelection.

Over the years, my enthusiasm for the integrative movement was put to the test. I perceived a sort of Euro-mania taking over in the nineties, as the Brussels bureaucracy grew to mammoth proportions. The eventual membership of twenty-eight countries struck me as being a bit over the top. I was also skeptical about the benefits of a common currency to such disparate economies. On my visits to the Netherlands, my most stimulating and informed source was my friend Max Weisglas, a former chief press officer of the Dutch Ministry of Economic Affairs and later professor of European studies at the universities of Amsterdam and Antwerp. Max was a staunch supporter of most of the decisions made in Brussels. But I could not get rid of the nagging question: how does one reconcile the cultures of Finland and Spain? Or of Germany and Greece? It just seemed too farfetched to believe that a United States of Europe could become a reality on the model of the United States of America. The States in the American union have a major advantage in that their citizens speak the same language. The U.S.A. also happens to have one Constitution, a federal legal system and a single Internal Revenue System. The EU has twenty-four official languages and twenty-eight legal systems.

I used to visit a client headquartered in a town half way between Antwerp and Brussels. The town was in the Flemish speaking part of Belgium. The client, a multinational corporation, had located its administrative and research facilities in a complex of buildings housing well over a thousand employees. The company used English in all its written communications. One day the town government issued a decree: all communications were henceforth to be in Flemish. In the ongoing Flanders-Walloon turf war, Belgium was gripped by an extreme form of language nationalism. When Edith went shopping in Brussels, the French speaking capital, a sales clerk pretended not to understand her when she addressed him in Dutch (a close relative of Flemish). Fifty years later, the positions have hardened further, and the partition of Belgium into two sovereign states seems more likely than ever. If a country like Belgium cannot overcome the language barrier, what hope is there for the entire continent? On a wider front, resentment of the European Union has been growing in a number of countries, with increasing calls for withdrawal. It makes me sad to think that the grand experiment may yet come unraveled.

8

/////////////////////////////////////

AT HOME WITH THE HILLS

During our first few years in Europe, I flew to New York at least once a year. Those were the days when air travel was still a pleasant experience, with the airlines falling over themselves to offer business travelers every comfort and courtesy. On transatlantic flights I would climb a small ladder and get a good night's sleep in the area that is now the overhead bin. One Pan Am night flight back from New York landed without my luggage aboard. A few hours later a messenger showed up at my house with a package containing fifty dollars "for your immediate needs," even though I was home. Also a handsome pen set with a note from the airline "to facilitate your writing us an angry note."

When Edith accompanied me, John and Elena Hill always insisted that we stay in the guestroom of their Park Avenue apartment. Our visits were generally the pretext for a dinner or cocktail party at the Hills'; I always looked forward to these, since they were bound to be entertaining.

As a couple, John and Elena were a study in contrasts. John

was a taciturn, down-to-earth Midwesterner; Elena a lively, mischievous former stage actress of Armenian descent. She was a friend of the film director Elia Kazan; her greatest claim to fame was playing the role of the mother in his movie *America, America*. Elena had one daughter and had recently adopted a little boy, but John made it clear that he was not very interested in children. They were Elena's department.

Edith and I adored Elena; she was a breath of fresh air, a hostess who liked to shake up what could otherwise have been rather stuffy occasions. She frequently pretended to be exasperated: John had again phoned that afternoon, she'd complain to Edith, shaking her head, to tell her he was bringing eight, twelve or even seventeen strangers home for dinner. Elena did not cook; she relied on a loyal maid. But she knew how to get back at John when she felt taken for granted. She thought nothing of showing up in an old sweater, proudly pointing out the moth holes in her sleeve to some impeccably dressed lady. One evening, presiding over a large group around the dinner table, John asked Elena, "Isn't there any bread, dear?" In America in those days, bread meant Wonder Bread, the doughy white mass that could easily be mistaken for a wad of paper napkins. Elena replied with a theatrical toss of the head that she would *never* have that junk in the house. All conversation stopped. The new client being wooed was the American Bakers Association.

For John Hill, entertaining at home was more than a business courtesy; it was a way of life. To host a few of his favorite associates, family friends, clients, or just interesting new contacts at his table or in his library, gave him an opportunity to absorb information and sound out new ideas. He was an excellent listener, with the ability to store a wide range of opinions expressed by industrialists, economists, bankers, and journalists of his acquaintance. Elena's contribution to the mix included movie actors, theater people, musicians and artists. An autographed portrait of the actor Charles Laughton was prominently displayed on the desk in the library. John was a great lover of music, and when I was in New York he often invited me to accompany him to a concert at Carnegie Hall, or whatever show was then the smash hit on Broadway. Staying in his apartment meant being required to join him on his daily forty-block walk downtown to the office. Lugging a heavy briefcase full of European reports, I would suggest taking a cab; Hill's standard reply was that I could do with the exercise. Walking, he declared, was healthy, and good for me.

Both in the office and at home, John was a man of few words; a withdrawn character, often extremely hard to read. A proud Republican and non-dogmatic libertarian, he counted Senator Robert Taft among his friends, but was reticent about his own political views. He had founded a group called "The Wise Men," which gathered once a month for dinner at the University Club. Its members were the senior public relations executives of America's largest enterprises. Invited speakers ranged from ex-presidents, mayors and other politicians, to well-known journalists and columnists. He also regularly hosted dinner parties for a smaller circle that included Robert Bartley, the editorial page editor of *The Wall Street Journal*. The talk was generally about the economy or national politics. Although cagey about his own views, John was very good at capsulizing what had been discussed. One night, when I had been invited to give a talk about what was happening in Europe, the discussion moved to the views of Friedrich Hayek, the Nobel Prize winner and high priest of individualism. Professor Hayek would have felt completely at home with Hill and company.

My own political views were middle-of-the-road and quite moderate. I had not followed in my father's footsteps. He was a Socialist, one of the great multitude of workers and small business owners fighting their way out of economic hardship. I grew up to be a European liberal, unattached to any particular party. The adherents of Europe's Liberal parties had much in common ideologically with American Independents; never drifting far from the center, swinging either left or right depending on which of the candidates or centrist platforms they found most appealing. In practice I usually found myself leaning slightly to the left. It was a prevalent post-war European stance. I abhorred extremists, whose views, when implemented, invariably led to disaster. Instead, I supported the U.S. politicians who could articulate an intelligent, long-range view of America's indispensable role in the world. At Hill & Knowlton headquarters, naturally, opinions came in all shades. Hill and my predecessors had all been rightwing allies and supporters of the early 20th Century industrialists; on my own internal board in the 1970s, I suspected that most voted Democrat.

At one dinner party at the Hills', I was baffled when two guests sitting near me began to discuss and compare the guns they owned. They were astonished to hear me confess that I had never owned a weapon, and did not intend to ever acquire one. Surely I had learned to use one when I was in the Army? I told them that when I was drafted, on Java, I was indeed trained to use a rifle, but I hated having to handle the thing, and wound up bribing a comrade to clean it for me. Even though I recognized that the U.S. was a violent country, I never got used to the belief held by many Americans that it was their birthright to possess as many guns as they liked. To deny that gun ownership was linked to a higher murder rate than elsewhere in the Western world was equally perplexing. On this score I remained a European my entire life. Debating the issue felt treacherous, however. I was well aware that H&K had at least one gun manufacturer as a client. I justified my avoidance of the subject by telling myself that, just as in the case of the legal profession, every company was entitled to have its voice heard in the court of public opinion.

In her Park Avenue apartment, Elena's friends from the theater world mixed easily with members of John's peer group. It was a meeting of two worlds: John's senior associates, solid and somewhat stodgy, and Elena's friends, lively and Bohemian. At one of the more select get-togethers in the barn of their weekend farm in Patterson, NY, Elena and an actor neighbor invented dialogues, and put on riotous improvisations that were heartily applauded.

It was in the consumption of alcohol that Edith and I discovered a fundamental difference between Europe and America. Cocktail hour at the Hills' could be a rather lamentable affair. It was not only the men who indulged in gin, Scotch, bourbon, or vodka; so did their wives. In one corner of the room, the men stood around with drinks in their hands talking business, politics and baseball; in the other, some middle-aged ladies, seated on a couch with Edith, took turns patting her hand or clutching her arm. Two of them, married to two of my senior bosses, were inebriated and, we concluded, were probably alcoholics. Edith never understood whether their behavior was meant to persuade her to join in the drinking, or whether it just expressed their need to feel close to a younger, sober person. John Hill did not participate in the drinking; he limited his consumption to one or two beers at night. At the office he had laid down the rule that no liquor was to be served at lunch. Elena, like Edith, did not really drink. I began to understand, however, that alcohol—hard liquor, as opposed to the European style of wine with dinner—was an important ingredient of the Madison Avenue lifestyle in the 1950s and 60s. Business and advertising executives needed their three-martini lunches, and on weekends at the country club, great quantities of bourbon on the rocks. I had never encountered drinking on such a scale anywhere in Europe.

In the 1970s, when I was the firm's CEO and living in New York, I was still frequently confronted with the issue of excessive alcohol consumption. One of the people closest to me, a highly creative and fast worker, would leave the office every day at noon in order to visit his bank. Except that on the executive floor everyone was well aware that "the bank" was actually a bar located on the ground floor of our building. Two of our other most productive executives, first-rate writers and fast friends, each had their own battle with alcohol. One drank too much at lunch and became belligerent in the afternoon; we would tell him to go finish his work at home. He was able to meet every deadline, and the quality of his work never faltered. He was just one of those people who delivered a superior product even when away from the office. Another of the big drinkers came to a meeting unable to conceal that he'd had one too many, jeopardizing his relationship with the client. We sent him to rehab. Several months later his daughter came to thank us for having saved his career; the client had put him back on the account. Ironically, the Licensed Beverage Institute, the trade association of the liquor industry, was one of our clients.

9

///////////////////////////////

CITY OF POLYGLOTS

After seven meager years, John Hill's "Folly" in Europe seemed finally to be turning around. We had entered a new phase of growth, and greater demand by our American clients for Europe-wide services. During a visit to New York in the fall of 1959 a decision was made to establish the European headquarters in Geneva. Geneva was a logical choice: it was fast growing as a major hub for multinational corporations, and the European site of the United Nations and its related agencies.

Edith received the news with mixed feelings. We had recently bought a new, larger townhouse in The Hague, near my office, within walking distance of a good school for the children. For Edith, it was a return to the city of her birth, where she had lived until the age of seventeen. At the same time, she could not entirely disagree with me that four years in the Netherlands was just about enough. She recognized that the narrow provincial atmosphere was getting on my nerves. Holland seemed to be standing still, the social and political climate reminiscent of the 1930s. Conversations about the war with family and friends were endless. Now, fifteen years after the end of the war, tongues were finally beginning to loosen: whereas at first our countrymen had avoided talking about what they'd been through during the war, the subject had now been hauled out of the closet, to be rehashed ad nauseam. Everything else people talked about had a decidedly narrow, provincial focus as well. Having lived in America and France had given us a broader perspective. To me, Holland was small-minded and boring most of the time. It made me feel constricted. I needed a new horizon.

But moving again, to yet another new country, was a major undertaking, and the bulk of the work, the packing and planning, fell on Edith. My job kept me on the road for much of the time, and even when I was home I wasn't much help. Male chauvinist that I was, I gave little consideration to her feelings. In those days, the wife and children were expected to follow the husband and father; his career came first. There was no arguing. We sold the house in The Hague and, after a tearful and somewhat melodramatic leave-taking from my parents, set out for Switzerland on January 1, 1960—the first day of the new decade, on what I hoped would be another auspicious new start.

It was cold and rainy, just as it had been when we had first arrived back in Europe. Edith and the children were a bit teary on leaving the familiarity of our home behind, but excited, too, about the new adventure. We drove out of town in our new Fiat 2100, packed with suitcases and toys. We stopped for the night in Brussels, in the very same Hôtel Atlanta where we had spent the night upon disembarking in Cherbourg five years earlier. The next day it was on to Dijon and eastern France, across the snowy Jura mountain range and into Geneva, the idyllic Swiss city on Lake Léman bordering France, with its medieval "old town" and proximity to the skiing slopes of the Alps. Exhausted from the long drive, we finally arrived at the Hôtel Century, in the center of town, where an efficiency suite with kitchenette would be our temporary abode.

The first order of business, as always, was to find a proper place to live. We had no clue where or how to begin. During our first week I was mostly tied up in meetings, and preoccupied with my quest for office space. Edith took charge of finding an apartment. She set out on a wintry day along the elegant Rue du Rhône shopping street with the intention of visiting the American and Dutch consulates to obtain information on real estate agents. Attracted by the window of a furrier, Edith was tempted inside by the *patron*, who insisted she try on several glamorous coats. She soon realized that they were out of her price range, but nevertheless kept browsing. That night she sheepishly confessed that she had been so dazzled by all the luxury stores that by the time she had reached the consulates, they were closed. She began the search in earnest the following day, however. The past four years in our home country had caused our Dutch *gestalt* to creep back into our thinking; we were looking for a cozy ("*gezellig*") home. The places Edith was being shown were rather forbidding and gloomy, reminding us of our year in Paris. Finally she found a furnished apartment on the Avenue William Favre, across the street from a park where the children could play. Although rather dark and cramped, it was the best we could get at short notice.

It was luck that led me to an office building under construction in the center of town, one block from the boulevard along the lake. The owner of the building on Rue des Pierres-du-Niton was a local architect. He offered me an interesting proposition. Under Geneva's tax regulations, certain tax advantages accrued to the owners of commercial buildings if they set aside some space for residential purposes. If we took a lease on a third-floor office suite, we could have the penthouse apartment covering most of the top floor, with a winding staircase leading up to an enormous rooftop terrace. It had a spectacular view of the lake and its famous Jet d'Eau fountain, with the Jura mountains in the distance. It would be ready for our family in a few months. It was an irresistible deal, especially since the rent was very affordable.

At the end of the Christmas vacation the children set off for their first day at their new school. We had heard good things about the International School of Geneva, the first of its kind, with a history dating back to the 1930s. The school, known as *Ecolint*, exemplified the cosmopolitan character of the city. Dozens of nationalities were represented in the student body, although over half of the students were American. Their parents worked for the U.N. and other international organizations, or banks and multinational corporations. The school had a French side and an English side; not knowing how long it would be before we were called back to New York, we decided to enroll the girls in the English section. We were concerned how the girls would adapt, since the twins had completely forgotten the English they had spoken as toddlers in New York. Now they would have to learn French as well. Three-year-old Jessica came home from her first day at the United Nations nursery school complaining, "They all *know* how to speak Dutch, they just *refuse*." We needn't have worried: all three girls became fluent in both English and French within a few months.

On prior visits to Geneva I had asked the advice of Maître Merkt, a well-established local attorney. Merkt had laid out for me the pros and cons of incorporating our firm, and the do's and don'ts of temporary residency. It was a time when the *Canton de Genève* (the province of Geneva) was eager to attract foreign companies; the authorities were offering tax advantages to newcomers. These were for the most part subsidiaries of American, British, European, Near Eastern or Japanese corporations. Most brought along with them a considerable number of non-Swiss employees. The diverse teams of managers and their staffs were given the required residence permits. Their Swiss hosts never went so far, however, as to regard them as anything but as aliens. Although this foreign workforce represented a melting pot of nations, the top jobs at companies like Dupont, Procter & Gamble, Caterpillar, and Chrysler, were largely held by U.S. nationals. With my Dutch nationality, I was the exception.

Our prospects in Geneva had looked promising from my office in The Hague, but turned out to be less auspicious than expected. Despite the preparatory trips I'd made to the U.S. that had seemed most encouraging, several long-term client arrangements I had been counting on never materialized. I was back to depending on ad hoc assignments, without the stability of a retainer. The exception was one client, the American Cyanamid Company, a diversified chemical and pharmaceutical company (long since taken over by the pharmaceutical giant Pfizer). American Cyanamid had just opened a research facility in Geneva; we assisted in the preparation and dissemination of press materials for the opening.

One of Cyanamid's senior executives was General Anthony McAuliffe, a hero of the 1944 Battle of the Bulge. After retiring from the military, he had joined the company as a vice president. One of his roles was to advise managers both in the U.S. and abroad in government relations, which meant encouraging them to reach out to local officials.

I was skeptical of retired generals or admirals who had taken on second careers in business. Were the companies that hired them buying useful contacts, or hoping to acquire technical insights? Or was it just the prestige of their rank that made them a catch? My cynical view of retired military brass had been forged in The Hague, when a former Dutch Army Chief of Staff had invited himself to have lunch with me, at my expense. General Kruls, a controversial figure in the Netherlands because of his political skirmishes with members of Parliament, had been retained as adviser to a large American financial institution. His purpose in seeing me was to ask whether any of our clients would like to avail themselves of his services, and whatever unspecified benefits those might confer. It was very clear that his main motivation was to supplement what he considered an in-adequate government pension. The admiration I felt for Generals Eisenhower, Arnold, Patton, Montgomery, and

Nimitz, was one thing; it did not mean that all generals were an automatic fit or asset in the private sector.

General McAuliffe was a small, amiable man who reminded me of my father. He had made quite a name for himself in the Battle of the Bulge, for having famously said "Nuts!" to the Germans' ultimatum of surrender during the 1944 standoff in the Ardennes. I was to accompany the American general to the Belgian town of Bastogne, which was honoring him for his defense of the besieged city sixteen years earlier. The streets were hung with banners and schoolchildren lined the route waving American flags. The Mayor, proudly wearing the long chain of office draped across his chest, gave an interminable speech in French, praising and thanking the General. My role was to act as interpreter. The mayor's flowery commendation dragged on so long that both the General and I began to feel exhausted. On the return trip McAuliffe confessed to me that it wasn't actually he who had coined the famous "Nuts" reply. It was one of his colonels who had suggested it, although it was the General who was given the full credit.

Cyanamid had sales and manufacturing facilities throughout Western Europe and was for several years the major source of our fee income in Geneva. It came as quite a shock, therefore, when a few years into this comfortable relationship, our client decided to reduce the consulting and operational budget allocated to us. Our budget was cut by eighty percent—a heavy blow, endangering our very survival. The news reached me on a beautiful summer evening while we were dining at the home of Swiss acquaintances. Gazing out over Lake Geneva, for a moment I lost my bearings. I was going down—hurtling toward the earth like a Spitfire fighter pilot, I thought, the only one in the squadron to be shot down in a dogfight with a German *Messerschmitt*. I was going to be sent home in defeat, a loser; I didn't know what I was going to tell my family, friends or colleagues. A few anxious weeks followed. I felt thoroughly defeated. But just as I had in other dark moments in my life, I shocked myself back into a better frame of mind by reminding myself of my years as a POW slave. There was no comparison between what I had experienced then and this temporary setback. I forced myself to look forward; to pick myself up and start again. John Hill remained staunch in his support. He did not ask me to close up shop, and over the next few months enough new business started coming in to compensate for the loss of this one major client. Never again would I risk keeping all my eggs in one basket.

My staff was miniscule. It consisted of Gwyneth Jones, my Welsh secretary, and Walter Pielken, a young Swiss broadcast journalist who had come looking for me upon reading the announcement of Hill & Knowlton's arrival in the paper. But within a few years we had grown into a larger, international team: one French-American executive, one Englishman, one Italian, two French-Swiss, a Swiss-German accountant and a couple of secretaries. The business was thriving. From our Rue des Pierres-du-Niton offices we coordinated the European assignments for a growing client list, performed by a network of now wholly-owned H&K subsidiaries in the capitals and business centers of Western Europe. It was a busy life: I was traveling fifty percent of the time. Geneva was a convenient, centrally located European hub.

I found myself guiding the American managers of European subsidiaries to adjust to the foreign culture in which they now operated. It was obvious to me, but not always to the American executives, that government structures in France, Germany and elsewhere were totally different from what they were used to back in the United States. The Hoover Corporation, for example, was nervously operating a plant in Lyon at a time when the Communists were a dominant influence in that part of France. Somehow, the management had allowed the factory to become neglected, rundown and dirty. This in no way fit the image of a modern American corporation that was all about keeping one's house spotless. Perhaps the reasoning was that in a poor neighborhood, you had to blend in. I suggested that a fresh coat of paint might improve morale and boost output. And so it did.

Geneva's citizens and their expatriate guests did not mingle much. Very few foreigners integrated into the *Suisse Romande* (French-Swiss) community. According to a Swiss neighbor, one of the few locals we got to know and who often invited us to his home for dinner, it was all a matter of numbers. One out of every five residents in our Canton is a foreigner, he said. How would *you* feel if twenty percent of your country's population was there on a temporary basis, and a good proportion of them did not bother to learn to speak the language? And yet Geneva managed to live up to its reputation as a cosmopolitan city with a largely tolerant and hospitable attitude to foreigners. The Swiss were savvy enough to appreciate the influx of foreign money through taxation and consumer spending. The expatriates, for their part, were content with life in the city, and found it a most civilized environment.

The prudent Swiss authorities did like to be assured, however, that the foreigners were not going to cause any trouble. They kept an eye on us; a wary eye at that. At one dinner party I was seated next to a middle-aged Swiss I had not met before. After being introduced, I began with the standard exchange: What do you do? Instead of a straightforward reply, my dinner companion said: "No need to tell me what *you* do. I have read your dossier." Later, our host told me that his guest was the head of the *Office des Etrangers*, the police department that kept tabs on every foreigner in the city. That information made me rather leery about my hosts' views on civil liberties. Maybe the attitude to foreigners was a little less tolerant than I'd thought.

Notwithstanding such discoveries, I developed a healthy respect for many of the Swiss institutions. First and foremost among these was the Referendum. On Sundays the citizens regularly went off to the polls to vote on issues that could seem quite trivial to foreigners. These ranged from traffic regulations to the tariff to be raised on imported apricots from Italy. I admired the Swiss adherence to the rule of direct democracy. I was also impressed by the loyalty the Swiss felt toward the canton to which they belonged. The system in which the twenty-six cantonal governments of the Swiss Confederation called all the shots, except in foreign and defense policy, seemed an excellent way to run this mountainous country. Despite the competition between the French-Swiss and German-Swiss, there was a palpable national loyalty, which was also expressed in the annual call-up of all able-bodied men under fifty for a three-week military training session. Each reservist kept his uniform, weapon and a box of ammunition in a closet at home. Thus one of the aspects of doing business in Switzerland was that Swiss employees had to be given time off for their military service. One of our employees would bring his army rifle to the office. Two decades after the end of World War II, the country seemed to be as combat-ready as ever. There was a nuclear fallout shelter in the basement of our building—a requirement for all new construction—and every household was charged with keeping a specified emergency store of food staples such as flour, sugar and rice. We were told to be prepared for the *Inspecteur de la Défense Publique* to pay us a visit some day, to check that we were in compliance. I told Edith not to worry: we had plenty of wine in the cellar. All this in spite of the fact that Switzerland had seen little combat in its long history, since it had remained neutral in both world wars. Some think that Hitler had little appetite for invading such difficult, mountainous terrain, and had therefore left it alone; it is more likely that it was a combination Switzerland's economic concessions to Germany and pure luck (the Normandy invasion and the Russian front demanding all of Germany's resources) that spared the country from a Nazi occupation.

I was well aware of the dubious roles the Swiss government and its banking community had played during that war, each in its own inimitable fashion. Switzerland, cleverly, had known how to walk both sides of the street. Some of our friends, fleeing the Netherlands, had found a safe haven there. But we also knew several Dutch Jews who, after a long, circuitous and hazardous escape route, had been refused entry at the Swiss border. One of them did make it on the second attempt. It had been a costly affair for him: he'd had to pay the French guide who led him over the Alps a small fortune not once, but twice. The escort had finally managed to smuggle his refugee client back into Switzerland, where the authorities had agreed to let him stay only after another friend vouched to guarantee his living costs. Many were not as fortunate: they were driven back, straight into the arms of German Army patrols or French collaborators.

Furthermore, Switzerland's banking secrecy law, which gave the banks an excuse to withhold pre-war deposits from the heirs of Holocaust victims for far too many years, created a lot of bitterness around the world. It was a wound that festered for decades before it was finally resolved, a full sixty years after the war. On balance, however, it appeared that many, if not most, Swiss citizens were more tolerant than their political and financial bosses. At the time when the struggle over the secret bank accounts was in the headlines, a young taxi driver in Zurich told us that he was part of a group of students who collected money to give to a Jewish organization because they were ashamed of the bankers' attitude. We knew a Swiss banker who had belonged to a group of volunteers that had set out for England and the U.S. early in the war to join the struggle against the Nazis. Living in a country that upheld strong democratic principles, was composed of countless isolated mountain communities, and accommodated four official languages, had given the Swiss a greater sense of self-sufficiency than many of their neighbors.

While the *Genevois* welcomed the influx of an international elite and the economic benefits these strangers brought with them, they were not as gracious to the imported labor, the workers who swept the streets, washed the dishes, and built the infrastructure. Like the rest of Switzerland, the city was prosperous, composed largely of the wealthy and middle class, people with little inclination to get their hands dirty. The jobs required to keep the city afloat were filled by foreign workers. When we had first arrived in Geneva, these came from southern Italy; in the latter part of the decade the majority were from Spain and Portugal, while nowadays the workers come from the former Yugoslavia, Albania or Turkey. These migrants were issued permits that allowed them to stay as guest workers for a period of nine months. When the permit expired, they were required to return to their country of origin. They could come back again the next year, to start the process all over again. But the imposed three-month hiatus gave the authorities close control over the working-class immigrants. It was not a hospitable place to bring your family. If you weren't gainfully employed you were sent home. After a number of years, foreign laborers could in theory apply for a so-called C Permit, allowing them to reside in Switzerland permanently. However, the barriers to citizenship were almost insurmountable, and apparently remain so to this day.

Edith and I moved among several different social circles: American transplants, employees of the recently arrived multi-national companies, Dutch expats, and various groups of international scientists, diplomats and civil servants. Geneva, the historic home of the League of Nations before the war, now hosted the European headquarters of the United Nations, the World Health Organization (WHO), the World Trade Organization (WTO), the International Labor Office (ILO), the International Telecommunication Union (ITU), and the European Organization for Nuclear Research (CERN). There were over forty large international bureaucracies based in Geneva.

Many of our social contacts were established through the intermediary of our three children. The parents of their friends became our friends. These included two nuclear physicists, an ILO lawyer and an American neighbor who posed as a diplomat but whom we suspected of being a CIA agent, which was confirmed to us forty years later.

Our friends were for the most part in their late thirties to mid-forties. Fifty-year-olds were rare, and were considered "ancient". The Dutch community did count two such elder statesmen, however: long-term residents Adriaan Pelt and Willem Visser 't Hooft. Receptions at Pelt's home in Hermance, on the lake just across the French border, were less boisterous than the parties of our usual crowd. Pelt, who had been present at the birth of the United Nation as deputy to Trygve Lie, the U.N.'s first Secretary General, had held the post of U.N. High Commissioner for Libya, and had helped draw up that country's constitution. Amongst ourselves we called Pelt "King of Libya". Willem Visser 't Hooft was the founding Secretary General of the World Council of Churches, which brought together 300 Christian denominations from all over the world. He was a rather aloof and stern looking gentleman, always dressed in black. He had spent the war years in neutral Geneva, where he had been able to act as liaison between Dutch resistance groups and the Dutch government-in-exile in London. He was thus a war hero without having risked his own skin.

Switzerland had for centuries been perceived not only as a bucolic idyll of mountains and lakes, cheese and cuckoo clocks, but also, through its bank secrecy laws, as a shelter for the fortunes of dictators, oligarchs and other billionaires. Geneva's Dutch community included a number of citizens who had moved there to escape what they considered predatory tax rates back home. A group of these wealthy tax-refugees had formed a luncheon club and baptized it "The last nickel." There were other distortions, most notably the IOS affair.

The Investors Overseas Services (IOS) was the brainchild of Bernie Cornfeld, who coined the famous pitch "Do you sincerely want to be rich?" to motivate his roaming mutual fund salesmen. Cornfeld had started IOS in the 1950s by persuading American service personnel in Vietnam and Europe to invest their paychecks in U.S. mutual funds; later his sales force grew to over 15,000, targeting expats all around the world. The company's financial products, including the lucrative fee-producing Fund of Funds, made a lot of people very rich at a time when the stock markets were soaring. Soon after IOS set up headquarters in Geneva, I received a call from one of my bosses in New York asking how we should respond to their request that we take them on as a client. I told him my instinct told me we had best decline.

Cornfeld had bought an old castle just outside Geneva, and made no secret of the fact that he enjoyed the life of a wealthy playboy. He struck many in the Geneva community, natives as well as imports, as a suspicious interloper. Many were convinced he was a conman, but others applauded his lavish lifestyle and welcomed IOS for the new money it brought to the canton and its environs. One of his gifts to the Swiss city was a culinary novelty: authentic pastrami on rye, served at a Jewish delicatessen that he opened at his mother's request, on the ground floor of the IOS office building. I remember that early on, one of our clients in London called to ask me about Cornfeld. I replied that I had no personal dealings with him, but his company seemed to be doing very well. Less than a year later the client sent me a case of wine to thank me: he had made a ton of money with his IOS investment, he told me, enough to buy a villa on the Costa Brava.

Over time, IOS and its affiliates came under political pressure and legal scrutiny in a number of countries including the United States, where the SEC opened an investigation of the company on numerous irregularities. In an attempt to regain some respectability, Cornfeld hired a number of dignitaries, including a British earl, a Swedish count, a former governor of California, and, most impressively, James Roosevelt, FDR's eldest son. Roosevelt, a former congressman, was the United States' delegate to UNESCO at the time. One of Roosevelt's first initiatives to burnish Cornfeld's tarnished reputation was to throw a lavish banquet for the city's top ambassadors, bankers, politicians and generals at the IOS company's lakeside villa. Much to Roosevelt's chagrin, the man of the hour, Cornfeld himself, never showed up. Things went from bad to worse for Roosevelt shortly afterward, when he was stabbed in the back by his third wife after she found out he was having an affair with the nanny.

It was said that in later years, IOS board meetings were marked by Bernie's anger and unease when it was suggested that the company should go straight and work under strictly legal norms. In the end the whole mirage blew up: Cornfeld spent eleven months in a Swiss jail for having defrauded some of his senior collaborators, but was acquitted of organizing and implementing his confidence game. The investors who had made a lot of money in the beginning lost it all in the end. I was glad to have steered clear of Cornfeld.

Our family made good use of the many advantages Geneva had to offer. The ski slopes were just a short car ride away, there were plenty of Michelin-starred restaurants in the vicinity for leisurely Sunday lunches, the airport was a fifteen-minute drive from home, and we enjoyed a stimulating social life. We felt fortunate to have stumbled upon the International School: the children were thriving there, and we were impressed with the educational system and the international outlook ingrained in the students. However, every utopian ideal of global harmony can have its ups and downs, and Ecolint was no exception. In this case, tensions had arisen between the English side and the French side. When the school was founded in the 1930s, it had been evenly divided. But thirty years later, owing to the great influx of American and English transplants, the students on the English side far outnumbered the French. The French and Swiss parents and teachers felt their existence threatened, while the English majority resented having to subsidize the much smaller French side. Two French board members resigned, and in the stormy debates that followed, the French parents complained that the school was becoming "Americanized". A vocal group of American and British business executives and international bureaucrats griped about a budgetary imbalance; the French-speaking parents felt that the defense of their national culture was at stake. It was war. The school auditorium became a battlefield: parents who practiced the niceties of diplomacy in their day jobs, turned into rabid partisans guarding their offspring's interests at night.

During one such rowdy and acrimonious meeting to elect new board members, I was involuntarily swept into the fray. I had been asked if I would run, but had declined to have my name put on the ballot. Someone called out my name from the floor, however, and I was elected by a unanimous show of hands. I was the only candidate to receive all English and French speaking votes. It must have been the fact that I was Dutch, the perception being that I was a neutral and conciliatory fellow, unlikely to worsen the already threatened *entente cordiale*. After a second bloodbath night that dashed any hope for a calm and realistic compromise, the board decided to invite Michael Blumenthal, then U.S. Representative to the U.N. Commission on International Commodity Trade, to act as arbiter. I was assigned to make the call; Ambassador Blumenthal accepted, and negotiated a solution that left most members of the board reasonably satisfied, although the most fanatical parental faction still evinced a bitter sense of frustration. (This was the same Michael Blumenthal who was later Secretary of the Treasury under President Carter. I was to encounter Blumenthal again when he was CEO of a succession of Hill & Knowlton clients.)

As a school board member I was drawn into a project that, looking back, is one that I am most proud to have been part of. The school had a top-class teaching staff, but some parents expressed frustration with the restrictive nature of the final exams. There were four different avenues to graduation: the Swiss Maturité, the French Baccalauréat, the British A Levels, and the American College Boards. That was fine if the student was interested in attending a British, French, Swiss or American university. But what if you were from Norway, Argentina, Nigeria or China? As an international career nomad, you might not be able to foresee where your next assignment would take you, or whether your children would have the right qualifications to pursue studies in their native country. Besides, preparing a student for one of these four national exams meant having to teach a restricted curriculum, rather than one reflecting a genuinely global outlook; and separating the students into national groups was counter to the principles of a truly international institution. For all of those reasons, the concept of the International Baccalaureate diploma took hold: a sensible idea that would some day allow its graduates to be eligible for admittance to any university around the globe.

I was asked to join a four-member committee to review the plans presented by John Desmond Cole-Baker, Ecolint's headmaster at the time, and Alexander Peterson, an Oxford University professor and expert in international education. Cole-Baker and Peterson were passionate in their pursuit of the idea. They had enlisted several of our daughters' teachers to help fashion a curriculum intended to encourage an understanding and appreciation of other cultures, languages and points of view. Our committee was enthusiastic about having our children serve as guinea pigs in a program that could lead to a breakthrough in international education. Harvard, Princeton, Oxford, and Cambridge were among the first universities to accept the exam as an entrance qualification.

Our committee meetings were held in the home of one of the members, the daughter of Linus Pauling, the Nobel Prize winner and promoter of vitamin C. The room was lit by dozens of candles of various sizes, which lent a mellow mood to the proceedings, far removed from the parental brouhaha in the school's auditorium. One of the challenges facing the fledgling program was the search for seed money. UNESCO had provided some early funding, but the teachers devising the tests and curriculum were basically doing it on their own time. In the 1960s, fundraising from individuals was not yet an accepted practice in Europe. Fortunately, an angel was found in the person of another board member, Georges-Henri Martin, editor of the *Tribune de Genève*. Martin also sat on the board of The Twentieth Century Fund, which came up with $75,000 in start-up capital. It was proposed that I should attempt to get some publicity for the new exam, but at this early stage the progress was insufficient to get the attention of the press. Later, when the program was somewhat more fully developed, it received funding from a number of governments, including the

Netherlands, Germany, the U.K. and Iran, as well as the Ford Foundation and other trusts.

Over the years, those modest, Geneva-based International Baccalaureate beginnings took off, turning into a worldwide success story. From a start that involved just a few students and a core of top admitting universities in the West, the IB is now widely used by nearly one million students in many thousands of high schools around the world (including my own grandson, Luca, who in June of 2015 graduated with an IB from the United Nations International School in New York). The participation by colleges and universities has kept pace. Globalization has brought with it the acceptance of the IB; it is not only a necessity for the children of international diplomats and businessmen, but regarded as a mark of distinction in the world of education.

Edith and I went back to Holland several times a year to see friends and family. My father died in Amsterdam at age sixty-seven of a massive heart attack. Even though he had never shown any interest in the Jewish religion, and the only times he had set foot in a synagogue had been at his own wedding and mine, the rabbinate assumed all responsibility for the funeral arrangements. I was expected to take part in the ritual washing of the body, cloaked in a white burial shroud. I washed his feet and contemplated the tallit, which we'd had to borrow for the occasion. I felt alien and rather a fraud, surrounded by a throng of bearded men chanting in a language my father had never learned. My mother continued to live a reasonably contented life until her mid-eighties, when she died of stomach cancer. Over the course of my lifetime, the critical attitude I'd had toward her as a teenager was replaced by deep appreciation for the mother who had stood for hours in the sweltering heat outside the barracks where I was imprisoned in Bandung just to get a glimpse of her son. During her final hours I was on a business trip, as usual. She drifted off peacefully in Edith's arms.

Our family's relationship to the Jewish community of Geneva was rather tenuous. Edith had a nostalgic hankering for Jewish traditions, and felt more attached to her Jewish upbringing than I felt to mine. At first we tried attending High Holiday services at Geneva's main synagogue, a strictly orthodox institution that was not especially welcoming to more liberal outsiders like us. The prayer book was traditional; the whole atmosphere too cool and distant for our liking. Meanwhile an English Speaking Jewish Community was founded, which practiced the kind of Reform Judaism that reminded Edith of her parental traditions.

One of the twins' best friends, Marian, was the daughter of Herb and Kate Katzki. Herb had devoted his life to helping Rumanian Holocaust survivors and other refugees through his work for the American Joint Distribution Committee; Kate worked at UNICEF and the U.N. High Commission for Refugees. One day, while on a walk on the Salève, a nearby foothill of the Alps, Marian slipped and fell to her death. It was the first great tragedy in the twins' twelve-year-young lives, and caused months of inconsolable sadness. In Marian Katzki's memory a theater program was started at the International School; the first play that was put on was *The Diary of Anne Frank,* with a talented Indian student in the title role. Otto Frank, Anne Frank's father and the family's sole survivor, made the trip across Switzerland from his home in Basel to attend the performance and meet the students. Many in the audience could not hold back tears, including Edith, who had befriended Mr. Frank's secretary, Miep Gies, in 1950, in the Amsterdam maternity ward. After the performance we felt privileged to be introduced to Mr. Frank, a sad but noble figure.

Through the Katzkis we also met Charles Jordan, Herb's close friend and boss. Jordan too had a long and distinguished record of helping refugees of the Holocaust and, after the war, aiding Jews living behind the Iron Curtain. On a visit to Prague in 1967, in the middle of the Cold War, he went out for a newspaper and never returned; four days later his body was found floating in the Danube. The motive and the identity of the murderer remain a mystery to this day. The Czech regime claimed to have thoroughly investigated his murder, but no one in the West bought that story. The Katzkis were devastated, naturally, by this tragedy; they won our respect and admiration for the way they coped with yet another terrible loss.

Most of the American executives we knew in Geneva spoke no French. Some did try to learn the language; others never bothered, even if they stayed for years. U.S. companies tended to select executives with the relevant technical, organizational, or marketing skills for stints abroad; language ability was deemed unimportant, even irrelevant. It made sense back home in the States, but did not always work out in practice. I heard a story that went around Procter & Gamble about a new marketing expert in its Munich office. The man sent over from the Midwest was asked by his new general manager about his knowledge of German. He answered that he didn't speak German but was fluent in Yiddish! I found it striking how few of the hundreds of American expatriates in Geneva had any interest in learning French. One of our acquaintances was proud to tell anybody who would listen that he had lived there for more than twenty years and did not understand a word of French.

The American expatriates were generally divided into two camps: those who loved Geneva and those who hated it. It was often the wives who had the hardest time adapting. Their husbands were occupied all day at work; the women were the ones who had to navigate the challenges of living in a different culture. In the 1950s and the 60s it was very unusual for executives' wives to work outside the home. One man who had been transferred from Morocco to Geneva was recalled to the U.S. after just one year. His departure was not related to any professional shortcoming on his part, but to his wife's mental health. The woman, who was liked by all who met her, suffered a serious nervous breakdown in Geneva. At least in Morocco she had had something to do—knitting blankets and scarves for the poor. Switzerland, however, had no poor population to speak of, and thus no need of her endeavors.

One day Edith received a call from Caracas; the woman on the line said that her husband was being transferred to Geneva and that a friend had suggested she ask Edith about life in our city. Edith responded by asking how well she had liked living in Venezuela? If she had liked her life out there, Edith said, then she would surely like the conditions in Geneva. If she thought Caracas was dreadful, she was bound to find Geneva equally disappointing.

By contrast, my energetic wife was determined to make the most of her time in Geneva. The opportunity to study under the famous psychologist Jean Piaget was irresistible. She enrolled in the University of Geneva to study with the great master. The august professor, in his trademark black beret, commuted to the university on an old bicycle. He would sit at the front of the lecture hall droning on about his difficult theories while at the same time correcting papers, rarely looking up to engage with the students. I tried helping Edith prepare for her exams, but gave up almost immediately. I found the professor's scientific jargon and Piagetian French hard to follow. Edith persisted, and drew a great deal of satisfaction from her studies, as well as her role as adviser and comforter to many friends who sought her wise counsel.

For the foreigners in Geneva, life wasn't always smooth sailing. Tensions roiled beneath the surface contentment. During our ten-year stay we counted seven suicides, including two of our Dutch acquaintances. One was an engineer working for a multinational company. He was divorced and slept in a trailer in the back yard of his former home. That is where his ex-wife found him when his office called to ask why he had not shown up for work. He had hung himself. The other was a member of our monthly bowling group, whose husband worked for an international Roman-Catholic organization. The news ricocheted throughout the community: she had set her house on fire with gasoline, killing herself and her three daughters while the husband was at work. Her friends speculated that, unable to keep up with the Joneses, she had given in to despair. She used to complain of penury: her husband's salary wasn't enough for her to keep up with the wealthy expat wives and their opulent life style.

Even in the darkest hours of my wartime imprisonment, suicide was not something I had encountered before. True, there were POWs who had given up the will to live, and many of those had died a painful death. But death had not been voluntary; I never witnessed nor heard of any Western soldier who had put an end to his life deliberately. So like everyone else in our circle, I was shocked upon hearing about the murder-suicide. Some of us wondered why, in the face of such a tragedy, the Swiss appeared to remain rather indifferent. Was it prejudice against foreigners? No, said one of our friends; to the Swiss, this was just another weather-related calamity, for they ascribed mood swings to the vagaries of the Alpine winds. There was the fierce but helpful north wind called the *bise* (as the saying went, *"avec la bise, lave ta chemise"*—when the *bise* blows, wash your shirt); and then there was the hot *föhn*, which came up from the south and was deemed responsible for a host of afflictions: depression, migraine, suicide, aggressive behavior and psychosis. The courts even marked the days of the *föhn* wind on the calendar, as a mitigating circumstance in cases of murder or assault.

Another difference I noticed in Switzerland was the work ethic. It seemed quite a bit more intense than in other European countries. Hard work and fierce attention to detail must be one of the main reasons for the success of the Swiss. Although perhaps not as gregarious by nature as some of their neighbors, the Swiss we got to know were devoted family people, socializing in small groups on their days off. They were fiercely proud of their country, the beauty of the scenery and the efficiency of their way of life. Sundays were for family expeditions—hiking in the mountains or leisurely lunches that could last for hours. Our Swiss friends Annie and Gusti showed us their favorite places—waterfalls, rock formations, where to pick wild berries or dandelion greens, and a very special Alpine meadow blanketed in jonquils in the early spring. They also taught us the secrets of the cheese fondue (which had to be washed down with *Fendant* wine, one was warned, otherwise the cheese would congeal in a hard lump in your stomach), and *raclette* cheese melted before an open fire, served with boiled potatoes and cornichons. Every weekend we would pack a picnic, pile into the car and explore the countryside, especially the bordering areas of France: the towns, villages, lakes, mountains, hillsides and plateaus of the *Haute Savoie.* Within Switzerland we picked daffodils and grapes, drank the unfermented young wine during the harvest festival, went boating on the lake, and gorged on great wooden bowls of strawberries and cream. Winters were for skiing and skating. It was a happy time for us, and a good place to see our children grow. We had a three-dimensional map of the region and would pore over it, tracing our fingers over the slopes to see how steep a certain hike would be. I liked to explore off-the-beaten-track places. One Sunday afternoon, at the end of a steep, three-hour mountain climb, we found ourselves high on an Alpine meadow, the only strangers in a crowd of revelers serenaded by a band of *alpenhorn*, where a cow adorned with garlands, crowned the "Queen" for its winning charms, lifted its tail and relieved itself, spattering dung all over the dancers on the wooden platform.

10

///////////////////////////////////////

A CONTINENT TOO FAR

In the mid-1960s, the Menzies Hotel in Sydney reminded me of an English railway station hotel. It was drab, with an unusually sulky staff. The coffee was more milk than coffee; the smell of stale bacon hung in the air. In all my travels, it was the only place where I was ever robbed: a gold tiepin which for decades had been an intrinsic part of my daily wardrobe went missing from my room. The memory still causes a lingering flash of irrational anger. Australia was one of those countries that I looked forward to visiting, and was always glad to leave. The place was simply too remote and too isolated.

Our firm had become associated with Eric White and Associates, the continent's largest PR firm, in the 1950s. Eric White had built an eleven-office operation spanning Australia, New Zealand, Singapore, Malaysia and Hong Kong. During the war, Eric had been press secretary to Prime Minister Menzies, and later remained an important adviser to Menzies' government and subsequent Prime

Ministers. Over the course of the years, "Mr. White", an introspective, taciturn stranger, became "Eric", a close friend and colleague.

Eric White was a larger than life pioneer, the doyen of his country's PR profession. Many of his former associates became successful practitioners in the field, with their own firms or in senior positions at competitors' companies. They socialized together, and became known in Australia as "the off-Whites".

The unpleasantness of the Sydney hotels contrasted starkly with the warm hospitality I often received in the Antipodes. An elderly New Zealand couple I met on a fifty-minute domestic flight promptly invited me to their sheep farm. They seemed genuinely excited to meet a foreigner. On a visit to the Adelaide office on Australia's South Coast, one of Eric's friends invited me to visit his vineyard. The wines were so delicious that I couldn't help swallowing enthusiastically, instead of sipping and spitting. Then, stepping outside hatless in the midday sun, I fainted. Some minutes later, having recovered, I felt well enough to ask my host to tell me more about the vintage that had knocked me out cold.

I realized that the warm welcome I received as a Dutchman was not extended to every foreigner. It was still an era of Australian chauvinism, offset by a hankering for the news from Britain, the motherland. The news programs dutifully reported the arrival times of the British Overseas Airways Corporation and Qantas flights from Europe. Many of the people I met were nostalgic about their stay in Earl's Court, a London neighborhood that was a favorite haunt of young Australians on their first tour abroad.

By the 1970s and 80s, the country seemed to have grown more mature and in many ways quite sophisticated. Sydney's spectacular new Opera house may have been the cause, or just a symptom. The food got better, with an international cuisine brought in by new imports from Greece, Italy and elsewhere; new art galleries opened. Racial prejudices persisted, however, including a strong antipathy towards the Japanese, a residue of the war. The country's immigration policy was very strict, and biased against all refugees from Asia. One of Eric's managers in New Zealand was a Maori. One night at dinner he confided that he hated all of them—his bosses, the clients, and his co-workers, all of them white. He described Caucasians as being outwardly condescending but racist at heart.

In the Japanese prisoner-of-war camps, the Aussie POWs had been the most positive and cohesive group, as compared to the Dutch or British. I used to envy them their camaraderie; they seemed to care more for each other, and interacted with a spirit of generosity that was alien to us Europeans. They also stood apart physically: broad-shouldered, rugged and tanned in wide-brimmed Aussie hats. Even when we had all shrunk to near-skeletal frames, they seemed to look more robust.

On a visit to the capital, Canberra, I made a startling discovery. I had time to kill before my flight back to Sydney, and the local manager suggested I might like to visit the War Museum. It seemed that almost every Australian city had is own war museum; not surprising, really, in view of the fact that the country had lost more soldiers per capita than their northern allies. The exhibition on show was entitled

131

Behind Barbed Wire and Bamboo, referring to the German and Japanese prison camps. A glass case displaying a hand-written, illustrated magazine caught my eye, "Created by POWs in 1944-45"... the original *Exile*, the very compilation that I had helped write and edit when I was in prison in Singapore! I could not believe my eyes. I was catapulted back to the time when I had worked on that volume, laboriously produced on the reverse sides of pilfered British Army documents. We had collected short stories and essays from the inmates, lavishly illustrated by the British cartoonist Ronald Searle and the Australian George Sprod. The two artists had gained fame after the war as contributors to *Punch*, the satirical London magazine. I asked to see the curator: was George Sprod still alive? How could I locate him?

One day later, back in Sydney, George Sprod, who had retired from his last job as cartoonist at *The Sydney Morning Herald*, came to the bar of my hotel. It was about forty years since we had last seen each other. We had grown into mutually unrecognizable, prosperous-looking gents, nothing like the skeleton-like wraiths who had worked together on *The Exile*. We spent the evening reminiscing about the struggle to put out a paper under impossible conditions, and raising a glass to departed friends.

One of the pleasures of my visits to Australia was the drive to Eric White's oyster farm in Foster, a couple of hours North of Sydney. Oysters were Eric's passion. He went out every morning in a small motorboat to his oyster beds; we ate his plump delicacies for breakfast, lunch and dinner. I discovered, however, that too many oysters, like too much wine, can give you a headache. Eric's wife, Peggy, was the daughter of a judge who had also served in World War II. Her father had left her a thin booklet with drawings by Ronald Searle depicting striking prison camp scenes, and portraits of the emaciated prisoners and their Japanese guards. It had been published by Cambridge University Press in 1946, in a very limited edition. Peggy gave her only copy to me; I was very touched by her gesture. Many decades later, in correspondence with Searle, I asked if he knew where I might get another copy. He replied that he wished he could find one himself.

Eric White died in 1989. He was remembered in the Australian press as a "dominant but shadowy figure." There was speculation that his offices in South East Asia were used as a cover for the Australian Security Intelligence Agency. As the two only non-Americans on the H&K Board, Eric and I were close, but I never had an inkling of Eric's Security Intelligence involvement. When Eric had opened offices in Kuala Lumpur and Penang, I'd assumed that it was his government connections that had helped reel in as advisers a member of the Malay ruling class, as well as former highly placed government officials. I am not likely to see the day when Australian government files will be opened and the true facts disclosed. I may be naïve, but even if the speculation about his connection with spy operatives turns out to have some truth to it, I'll never believe that Eric, my friend, was indeed the sinister figure some Australian journalists are now making him out to be.

11

////////////////////////////////

THE MAGNATES — KADOORIE, WALLENBERG AND THE AGA KHAN

Among the more interesting professional challenges that came our way was the city-state of Hong Kong, a British colony at the time. The new client was an alliance of the Hong Kong Chamber of Commerce and its counterpart, the Federation of Industries. The European Common Market had just slapped high tariffs on imports from Hong Kong, a severe blow, since textiles, toys and electronics exports to Europe were Hong Kong's mainstay. The seven countries of the European economic bloc were in no mood, however, to grant a special privilege to a colony of Great Britain, which was not yet a member (Britain did not join the EEC until 1973.) Our assignment was to devise and implement strategies to obtain an exemption from the new rules for Hong Kong, as distinct from the rest of the British Commonwealth.

The client had been recommended to us by Alan Campbell-Johnson in London. Alan and I flew to Hong Kong once or twice a year. There were no non-stop flights; en route, while the plane was refueling, we would be driven to a hotel in Bombay or Karachi, and after a good night's sleep, proceed on our journey. On one occasion our flight was delayed by more than twenty-four hours; arriving in Hong Kong, a car met us on the tarmac. We were whisked through immigration and customs and driven straight to the restaurant where, reeling with jetlag, I had to give a report on the current European situation as it affected our client's interest. One Englishman and some fifteen Hong Kong tycoons listened politely and asked a few questions. After dinner, the most senior of the group, a wealthy textile manufacturer, proposed a toast. The choice was either brandy or whiskey. I was informed that according to Chinese custom, when being so honored it was rude not to finish your glass *ad fundum*. I tossed down my whiskey in one gulp. But to my dismay it did not end there. One after another of my dinner partners raised a glass to me. I drained my glass more than a dozen times. I suspect that none of the others drank all of theirs. I did manage to uphold the honor of our firm, and perhaps my own, however, for apparently I refused to pass out. Back in my hotel room I was sick as a dog.

Hong Kong society was still quite hierarchical. The city's power brokers included the heads of the four main British-owned trading companies, each of which had fingers in many pies: trading, manufacturing, banking, real estate and all manner of other investments. The captains of industry lived in palatial villas and monumental mansions along a steep, winding road called The Peak. Some of the dinner parties at the homes of these nabobs were in tropical white tie. After dessert the ladies excused themselves and retired to the drawing room, leaving the gentlemen to enjoy their brandy and cigars. The talk was politics and horse racing, interspersed with ribald stories. One day I was invited to attend the Saturday races, in the box of Sir S. N. Chau, Hong Kong's most prominent Chinese businessman. He had been knighted by the Queen, and in acknowledgement of his status, he had the Number 2 Box at the racecourse; Box Number 1 was reserved for the British Governor. Almost all of the Chinese tycoons I met—textile, electronics and toy manufacturers, members of the core Supervisory Committee of the Federation of Industries—were originally from mainland Shanghai. They had settled here after 1948, fleeing Mao's victorious Communist army. I enjoyed their company, and, with the exception of my whiskey-banquet ordeal, never felt an uncomfortable cultural divide

Our main client contact in Hong Kong was Susan Yuen, the Secretary-General of the Hong Kong Federation of Industries; a seasoned businesswoman and forceful personality. A protégée of Sir Chau, she was tougher and more intelligent than most of her male counterparts in the Western world. This struck me at the time because in America and Europe, there were practically no female business leaders to speak of. In later years I heard that in anticipation of the ending of Britain's lease of Hong Kong, Susan had retired to Australia. Many of her compatriots had prepared for the Communist takeover by buying properties in other parts of the Commonwealth—Britain, Canada, or Australia.

Hong Kong's climate could be as sweaty as Indonesia's or Singapore's. The humidity was as uncomfortable as a hot summer day in New York. I found relief in the cool breezes of the fans in Kowloon's old-fashioned Peninsula Hotel, where I usually stayed. Air conditioning was a rare commodity back then. In later years I also stayed at the Mandarin (I attended its grand opening) and the Regency, where once, after a long transpacific flight, I was woken up every two hours by a solicitous but imperturbable butler inquiring if I had any wishes.

The Peninsula Hotel was owned by the Kadoorie family, part of the colony's elite, but still regarded by some as non-conformist outsiders. The two brothers who ran the dynastic enterprise were scions of a family of Baghdad Jews that had settled in Hong Kong two generations earlier. Their multi-faceted business interests included the city's main electric supply company, the Peninsula hotel group, and a number of other successful enterprises. During a party at Sir Lawrence Kadoorie's plush home, my host and I shared war experiences. The Japanese occupation of the city had been brutal, and especially rough on the Caucasian residents, he told me. His family had been interned in a prison camp, just as mine had been on Java. Kadoorie's father had died in the camp, and the Peninsula Hotel had been taken over by the Japanese for their headquarters. After the war the family's holdings in Shanghai were confiscated by the Communist government. Despite all that, Kadoorie managed to rebuild the family fortune. He asked me if I would like to see the experimental farm he and his brother had founded in 1951 to aid poor farmers, a project close to his heart. The following day he gave me a tour of the spectacular Kadoorie Farm and Botanic Garden at the foot of The

Peak, Hong Kong's tallest mountain.

At the other end of the spectrum from The Peak's mansions were the tower blocks being built in the New Territories, a vast area set aside for public housing. The general population of Hong Kong was not poor, but it wasn't prosperous either. Many inhabitants needed government support in order not to fall into poverty. The government had stepped in and provided the colony with good public education, medical care and housing. Although the colonial regime was proprietary, paternalistic and snobbish, it did provide excellent care. This had resulted in what was generally considered the highest standard of living in all of Asia, Singapore excepted. The population of Hong Kong was incomparably better off than the hundreds of millions Chinese on the mainland then suffering under the Communist dictatorship of Chairman Mao.

I spent most of my time in offices, or at lunch and dinner with our clients, but once in a while I succeeded in breaking away to get a more complete sense of the place. Talking to Chinese public servants, journalists, shopkeepers, university lecturers and bank employees, I found no great fear of the nearby People's Republic. However, Hong Kong's richest citizens, apprehensive about the future, had taken precautionary measures and were prepared to escape to Britain or Australia in the event of a mainland Chinese invasion. Meanwhile everyone was in favor of the status quo: let the British stay and keep the Communists out, was the consensus. My own sense of comfort in this Asian city was in sharp contrast to the malaise I felt visiting Japan, where I was constantly fighting off my mistrust about my hosts' motives, and a conviction that we would never see eye to eye. I realized that it was irrational of me, but in the company of Japanese I could not ignore the scars the war had left inside me.

A delegation from Hong Kong on a tour of Europe visited our Geneva office. It was led by Hugh Barton, the Taipan (chairman) of Jardine, Matheson & Co, one of Hong Kong's major trading houses. Barton, a tall, suave Englishman, was curious to see how the other half lived. Would it be an imposition, he asked, to ask to see our home? I phoned Edith to tell her that we would be having seventeen guests for dinner. Fortunately my unflappable wife was up to the task, and managed to pull together a last-minute buffet of French-Swiss specialties for a small army of Hong Kong business executives.

My travels sometimes took me in a more northerly direction as well. In the mid-1960s our company was put on retainer by the Wallenberg family, which entailed my flying from Geneva to Stockholm once a month. The Wallenberg group of companies, the largest family-owned business in Europe, controlled about ten percent of the Swedish economy at the time. The Wallenbergs had enjoyed a favorable tax arrangement with the government for decades. Their profits were channeled into various tax-exempt foundations, so that the family owed little or no tax. To non-Swedes this was a surprising concession, since Sweden's Socialist government had the reputation of being the most punitive tax regime in Europe. Apparently the government felt that the Wallenbergs' contribution to the nation's welfare was worth the special deal. Sweden's industry, heavily controlled by the Wallenberg dynasty, brought hundreds of millions of kronor to the state's coffers from Saab, Atlas Copco, Scania, Ericsson, Electrolux, S.A.S., and half a dozen other major companies. Our firm was engaged when it looked as if the tide might change. Prime Minister Tage Erlander, a moderate Socialist who had been in office since 1946, was about to be succeeded by Olof Palme, also a Social Democrat, but a more radical one. It was feared that a new government might introduce sterner measures. As it turned out, they needn't have worried; the family business went from strength to strength, and is said to control almost half of Sweden's wealth today. Prime Minister Olof Palme was assassinated during his second term in office; his murder remains a mystery to this day.

I made monthly treks to Stockholm's Grand Hotel, also owned by the Wallenberg family, to lead meetings with the heads of the PR departments of the companies involved. We set up communication channels and brainstormed defensive plans. One rather outrageous suggestion was that the Wallenbergs should simply buy the *Dagens Nyheter*, Stockholm's equivalent of *The New York Times,* and use it to control public opinion. The idea went nowhere, but the fact that it was even considered was proof, to me, of the family's financial clout.

Our meetings usually took place in a conference room of SEB, the largest national bank, another Wallenberg holding. After one such meeting, the most senior member of our group, Marcus Wallenberg's right-hand man, invited us to dinner at an elegant restaurant at the Opera House. There I was introduced to a Swedish drinking ritual that was uncomfortably close to the Chinese one I had experienced on one of my first trips to Hong Kong. I was offered a choice of three different kinds of Aquavit. After downing a glass for the *"Skol"* toast and pronouncing it excellent, I was told I would have to do the same with the next two Aquavits. Mindful of my alcoholic adventure in Hong Kong, I decided to sip.

The two reigning Wallenbergs were the brothers Marcus and Jacob. Marcus was the man we ultimately reported to. I only met him twice: a brief introductory handshake on my first visit to his domain, and on another occasion, at a rowdy Solstice celebration. Until that night, I had found the Swedish executives rather stiff and exceedingly formal. But I saw a different side of them at a Wallenberg party marking the Solstice, on June 21, the night the sun never sets in that part of the world. The revels went on all night; nobody even considered going to bed. By 4 A.M., as I was growing weary of the bright daylight, the heavy drinking and boisterous carousing, Marcus Wallenberg joined the party. He stayed for a while, then announced he was off to play a game of tennis.

The Wallenbergs had fared well in World War II. Sweden had been able to retain its neutrality, since the country was considered useful by both the Allies and the Germans. It possessed large quantities of raw materials of one kind or another that were crucial to the war effort on both sides. Marcus had maintained contact with and sold to the British; Jacob played a similar role with the Germans. It was good to deal from both sides.

Perhaps the best public relations asset Marcus and Jacob

could have wished for was their own late nephew, Raoul Wallenberg. If the Wallenbergs were let off easy in spite of Jacob's association with the Fascists, it was thanks to Raoul, famous for having saved a hundred thousand Jews during the war. As a diplomat stationed in Budapest, Raoul had managed to issue false papers to a great number of Hungarian Jews on their way to the gas chambers. Raoul's manifold activities included renting buildings hung with oversized Swedish flags to house hundreds of Jews; issuing an official-looking "protective pass" stamped with the Swedish crown, which ignorant German soldiers and Hungarian policemen mistook for a passport; and even personally pulling Jews out of trains bound for the death camps. In 1945 the Russians arrested him on suspicion of being an American spy. He was most likely shot in 1947, although decades of Swedish, Soviet and United Nations investigations have not been conclusive. He is remembered and honored as a truly exceptional war hero.

The Swedish PR campaign was a scattershot affair. We were directed by the Wallenbergs to keep the companies' efforts separate; each company had to show its individual value to the community in terms of employment and material support. So I flew around the country, visiting places like Helsingborg and Malmö. It was in Malmö, at the home of Saab's PR director, that I first had a taste of gravlax. I enjoyed it so much that the next morning my host sent me on my way with a large chunk of the raw marinated fish to take home, complete with the recipe. It became one of Edith's signature party dishes.

Nearly all of our clients retained our firm because they

had run into a predicament, or wanted advice on how to heal a wound that had festered over time. There were exceptions, however. When the Aga Khan asked me to come to his Geneva office, it was not about some sticky problem, but about promoting a project close to his heart: a luxury resort he was planning to build on the island of Sardinia. The Aga Kahn was nothing like what I had expected after hearing about his father, the playboy Aly Kahn, married to Rita Hayworth (their daughter was in the twins' class at the International School). This was a pleasant, gracious young man, a Harvard graduate with a British accent, whose offices were surprisingly unostentatious. He wanted us to set up an international promotion campaign for his upscale Sardinian vacation resort, aimed at the jet set. In order to do that, I needed to go there and check it out for myself. I took the night ferry from Genoa to Porto Cervo, where I toured the 35-mile, as-yet undeveloped Costa Smeralda, visited a couple of partially constructed hotels for the super rich, and was shown architectural plans for the luxury villas still to be built, including one for the Aga Kahn himself. Opulent yachts were moored in the small harbor, and there seemed to be little urgency to finish the project. I learned that the Aga Khan, whose family claimed to be descendants of the Prophet Mohammed, was one of the wealthiest religious leaders in the world. As the Imam of 15 million Nizari Ismailis, an Islamic sect spread across the globe, he was in the unique position of not having to worry about geographic boundaries in his activities as a philanthropist fighting poverty and disease, as well as building and restoring mosques all over the world. The family's enormous wealth was maintained through a system of tithing, in which each devoted follower who could afford it contributed twelve percent of his annual income to his spiritual leader. When the Aga Kahn's grandfather was alive, this tribute had famously taken the form of the Imam's own weight in gold.

12

//

A SHAGGY DOG STORY

In Europe, the PR profession remained generally misunderstood. By 1965, about ten years after I had first arrived in Paris, the number of large European corporations that had established PR departments was still small. The American multinationals had done a little better, although it was often good old Joe, the chairman's nephew, or some slightly-over-the-hill retainer, who was appointed the company's international PR director — a gracious way to avoid putting the old man out to pasture. The number of PR agencies had also grown, but at a very slow pace. It occurred to me that in Europe, PR was taking the same baby steps as the local newspapers in their coverage of business news. In Geneva, the two home town dailies, *Journal de Genève* and *Tribune de Genève,* would occasionally run a press release our office had issued on behalf of one of our clients verbatim —the only copy on the financial page besides the stock exchange tables. The English newspapers weren't any more advanced in this regard: when *The Times* of London started a business page, a crime reporter borrowed from the news desk was appointed its editor. Apparently the paper had no writer on staff with any economic or financial background.

Edith complained to me that when she had to explain what her husband did for a living, she found limited understanding and even less appreciation. When a six-year-old classmate of our daughter Jessica was asked what her dad did, she replied, "My dad does what Jessica's dad tells him to do". Her dad was the European PR director of Marathon Oil.

There was another PR man in Geneva with whom I developed a close relationship, although he was not a client. Byron Farwell worked for Chrysler International as their in-house PR Director. Byron and I found that we had much in common; our wives and children also hit it off. A World War II and Korean War veteran, Byron confessed to me that his day job was just to support his real vocation, which was writing historical non-fiction. The Farwells lived in a rambling old house with space set aside for an aviary filled with exotic birds. Another set of rooms had been turned into a museum where the children exhibited keepsakes from their travels; when Byron had to do research for a book, he took the whole family with him. He was writing a biography of Sir Richard Burton at the time, so the family accompanied him in tracing the itinerary of the famous 19th Century explorer in Africa. They regaled us with stories of their adventures, including a stop in Timbuktu, where because the water was unsafe to drink, the children had had to quench their thirst with bottled beer.

I have often been puzzled by management decisions that struck me as bizarre. Chrysler's decision to move its international HQ from Geneva to Australia was one. The Farwells did not go; they moved first to London and then back to the States. We visited them in Hillsboro, Virginia, a bucolic town where Byron served three terms as mayor. He was the author of over a dozen books—biographies and military histories, including *Mr. Kipling's Army* and *Queen Victoria's Little Wars*. Although Byron was a decade older than me and was certainly a far more prolific writer, I have often thought our lives followed a somewhat similar path, from war to peacetime Europe, from roaming businessman and citizen of the world to resident of rural, small-town America.

After some years in our penthouse aerie, living atop an office building had lost its charm. Edith and the girls advocated moving to a more residential neighborhood. Edith went out house hunting, and found a house on the lake in Vésenaz. It was too big and too far out of town for her, but the friend who accompanied her, Lo Polak, fell in love with it and declared she would take it if we didn't. Hans and Lo Polak were a Dutch-American couple we had met through our kids; their daughter Lynne was the twins' best friend. Hans worked for the aircraft manufacturer Grumman. They lived in a cozy house we had always admired in Chemin Fossard, near the girls' school; they moved out, and we moved in. We traded the apartment with a rooftop swing that gave you the sensation of flying out over the lake and the Jet d'Eau, for a charming cottage with a weeping willow drooping over the fence, a garden and an abundant cherry tree.

In Geneva my two indulgences were wine and cigars. On Saturday mornings I would visit Monsieur Burkhardt, our favorite old-fashioned neighborhood grocer on Place des

Eaux-Vives. He taught me to appreciate Burgundy wines and other fine and expensive delicacies. The other purveyor I loved to call on was Zino Davidoff, in his small cigar shop in the heart of the city. Zino, a natural salesman brimming with marketing ideas, had imported a genuine cigar maker from Cuba to sit in the shop window demonstrating the craft of rolling the tobacco. Zino persuaded me to switch from the common Dutch Sumatra leaf cigar to the royal taste of a genuine Havana. Zino had come up with the idea of naming his Cuban brands after famous Bordeaux wines. He told me he had recently come back from Cuba, where he had met Fidel Castro in person. Today, of course, the Davidoff brand is known throughout the world—another empire built on small beginnings. My family, unfortunately, was less keen on my cigars, and strongly protested whenever I lit up, especially on car trips. I eventually gave them up.

When clients came to town, we usually put them up at the Richemond, one of the world's great hotels, owned by the Armleder family, a dynasty of Swiss hoteliers. It was famous for hosting celebrities like Charlie Chaplin, Colette, Walt Disney, Henry Kissinger and Louis Armstrong. Besides its swank décor, the hotel had a number of distinctive features to recommend it. The bar always engaged a first-rate jazz pianist; Turkish coffee was served by a genuine Turk in native dress complete with fez; and I recall with fondness the heavy-set Lebanese gentleman who seemed always to be seated strategically at the bar attempting to sell someone a surplus Boeing 747.

John Hill, however, preferred to stay at the nearby Hôtel de la Paix, because it was "tranquil and old-fashioned," whereas the Richemond was "glamorous and fashionable." On one of his visits Hill caught a cold. Calling room service, he requested a peeled orange, his recipe against the common cold. After John repeatedly shouted his request into the phone in English, a waiter finally appeared at the door with six glasses of orange juice.

Hill's annual visits were always a high point, though not without drama. Hill was notoriously fussy about what he would or would not eat or drink. In preparation of his arrival, I once asked Edith to get some beer, which was Hill's only alcoholic indulgence. I remembered that he always asked for draft beer. On the day of the party, Edith called me in the office, upset and exhausted. She had gone all over town, but nowhere could she find the American beer called "Draft". I managed to procure a keg of the local brew. It seemed to make Hill happy.

On another of Hill's visits, I took him to see the Gillette plant in Annemasse, just across the French border. It was the year's first beautiful spring day, and the opening of the summer season. The plant's general manager and three of his associates had booked a table for lunch at *Père Bise*, a famous Michelin three-star restaurant, on nearby Lake Annecy.

The place had just reopened after its winter closure. The headwaiter recited a list of mouth-watering delicacies, then turned to Hill and asked what he would like. "Could you just bring me a little fruit salad?" John said. The headwaiter and the four French executives looked puzzled; John explained that he only ever ate fruit at lunchtime. Fruit salad and cottage cheese, actually. I tried to explain this American comestible, but cottage cheese was an item the French had never heard of. The request could not be filled. Still, the rest of us dug in to our meal enthusiastically. Hill just sat there picking at his fruit salad and sipping his lager for the three hours it took to finish the multi-course, fine-vintage meal. Fortunately the guest of honor's abstinence did not impair our hosts' enjoyment of their extravagant expense-account lunch.

About that time, our family acquired a dog. At the insistence of our children, and under considerable peer pressure from dog loving friends, Edith and I had finally given in. His name was Winston, his place of birth Ireland, and the trip to Switzerland by way of London turned out to be a traumatic ordeal. The little dog was en route for almost three days. We had no idea what had happened exactly, but decided that it was this trauma that had led to Winnie's hatred of all persons in uniform. Our postman soon got in the habit of tossing the mail over the fence from a respectful distance.

One night I invited Hill to the house by himself. I was looking forward to a quiet dinner entre nous, without colleagues, clients or friends. It was time, I felt, to broach the subject of a long overdue raise. After a pleasant dinner we moved to the living room to have coffee. John did not see Winnie sleeping in front of the couch, and stepped on him by accident. Winnie, snarling, jumped at our guest's throat. John, who did not like dogs, made his excuses and left. He flew back to New York the next day. Any discussion of my remuneration was put on ice.

Trips to the Far East, New York, the Midwest and West Coast, in addition to my constant wanderings around Europe, still accounted for over fifty percent of my time.

Edith rarely accompanied me; between looking after three children and her university studies, it was hard for her to leave home. But when she did, she saw to it that I didn't spend all my time in some stuffy office. Once, in Rome, an afternoon meeting was interrupted by a message from my wife. She was downstairs and had to speak with me urgently. I rushed out, fearing some terrible piece of news. Edith calmly introduced me to a driver who was to take us to see the Catacombs. I went back inside and announced the meeting was over.

Our man in Italy was Giancarlo Bertelli, a talented and enterprising young man who later became a television and film producer. He was married to Shanda Lear, a singer and daughter of aviation magnate William P. Lear, inventor of the Lear Jet. Shanda Lear bore her name, the product of her father's sense of humor, with good grace. We joked that her brothers should have been named Cava and Gondo; her grandfather, the comedian John "Ole" Olsen, of *Hellzapoppin'* fame, would have approved.

One day our Milan office had an unexpected visit from the fiscal police, the *Guardia di Finanza.* They carried out boxes and boxes of files. I was told not to worry: it was just business as usual. The Guardia assumed that we followed the common Italian practice of keeping two, if not three sets of books, in order to avoid taxation. They must have been disappointed that we only kept one set of books. Our files were quickly returned.

In the early 1970s, Edith and I found ourselves being fêted at a formal dinner at the Villa d'Este on Lake Como. The occasion was the awarding of an Italian order: I had been named *Commandatore* in the Order of Merit of the Italian Republic. I was not sure what I had done to merit my award. I was told that ten years earlier I had suggested to an American client that in the upcoming election Italy was not going to go Communist, despite the popularity of Palmiro Togliatti, leader of the largest Communist party in Europe. The client had a cargo ship with supplies on its way to Italy, when the results of a local election came in showing the strength of the Communists. The client was about to make the ship turn around and head back to the States when, according to legend, I made him change his mind. I was not wholly persuaded of the truth of this tale, and suspected that an Italian colleague, Dorio Mutti, whose wife was in that country's diplomatic service, was responsible for arranging the honor. (My cynicism about the merits of such awards dated back to 1958, when our work for Brussels World's Fair was nearing its end, and an official asked whether I was interested in a ribbon. "We have a railroad car full of the stuff that we have to get rid of." Embarrassed, I had declined the offer.) Some years after my elevation to *Commandatore,* I received a letter from the Italian government informing me that I had been promoted to *Grande Ufficiale,* a higher rank in the Order of Merit. This was highly undeserved, since I had not attended any of the Order's gala dinners in New York, or even tried to brush up my limited Italian language skills.

Spain was another world entirely. Separated from the rest of Europe by the high wall of the Pyrenees, it was a police state under the sway of Generalissimo Franco. Edith and I had toured the Basque coast in the late 1950s when there were few tourists of any kind. We had stayed in Zarautz, a beach town, where our hotel was totally run and staffed by women, and in San Sebastian, where our room overlooked a garden party thrown by the cardinal who lived next door. The splendor of that event, thronged with red-cloaked servants of the Church, contrasted sharply with the dark, poverty-breathing city of Bilbao, where our client BF Goodrich operated a dirty manufacturing plant. There was no hint yet of today's modern, gentrified Bilbao with its glittering Guggenheim museum. In the 1960s Spain was still a backward country. One of our clients, Marathon Oil, had a substantial interest in an oil refinery in La Coruna, the capital of Galicia, the province where Franco was born. On visits to Spain I shuttled between Madrid and La Coruna, with the occasional side trip to Barcelona on other client business. The Spaniards I met all acted rather subdued, and were reluctant to talk politics. I met only one man who had the courage to express his hatred of the Franco regime. But I knew that many people shared those feelings. The mood was one of dull resignation, like that of the occupied peoples of Europe and Asia during World War II. As for public relations, it had a very limited scope in Spain or neighboring Portugal. It took years, and the deaths of the dictators Franco and Salazar, for the profession to really take root in the Iberian peninsula.

In the late 1960s Geneva suffered one of its periodic attacks of xenophobia. Occasionally the canton woke up to the notion that it had simply allowed in too many foreigners. The reaction was an indiscriminate halt on the granting of work permits, whether the applicant was a business executive or a car mechanic. For our company this meant an end to the growth of our Geneva headquarters. Not being able to hire foreigners was a major headache for us. The number of experienced Swiss PR professionals in the entire country could be counted on one hand, and all of these were gainfully employed, extremely well paid and, in typical Swiss fashion, wedded to their employer for life. We were in a bind. To properly serve our multinational clients, we had no choice but to engage foreigners. Our multilingual staff was composed of British, French, Italian and Dutch citizens. We had only two Swiss nationals in our employ. All the others held temporary five-year work permits.

It was time for another move. A small exodus of American multinationals in the same predicament as us had begun. Many of them were setting up shop in London. We were willing camp followers, and were pleased to find out that Britain, although not yet a member of the European Union, welcomed foreigners. There was a personal upside as well: our twins had applied to English universities, and we liked the idea of not being too far away from them.

So after ten productive years in Geneva, we shrank our office there to a two-man operation, and set our sights on London. I found myself looking forward to the move. Ever the nomad, I never felt comfortable staying in one place for too long, and the idyllic, complacent life of Geneva was beginning to wear on me, with its lack of social diversity and stale business circles. The Geneva I was leaving behind was sterile, curiously provincial and inward-looking, in spite of being host to so many international organizations. I was not sorry to let it go. Yet like my wife and the children,

I felt that we were giving up what had been an important part of our lives. We had to leave behind our house, our many friends, the mountains and lake, our Portuguese maid Cioni, and the white cherry tree in the garden with the pink-yellow blossoms and wormy fruit. I told my family that it was healthy for us to move to London, where our children would experience what a bona fide, rugged city was like, with a full cross-section of a far more diverse society, with not only the affluent and middle class, but also beggars on the street.

13

//

IN THE CAPITAL OF A FALLEN EMPIRE

In contrast to our moves to Paris, The Hague and Geneva, when we'd had to fend for ourselves, London was the first relocation for which we received some support from my company. This was because London already had a Hill & Knowlton office in place. We had parted ways with Alan Campbell-Johnson some years earlier to set up our own London subsidiary. The office was headed by a PR veteran, Colin Mann. Colin was a thin, dapper gentleman some years older than me. He arrived at work every day with a spring in his step and a fresh carnation in his buttonhole, provided by his personal florist. Besides Colin, the office counted three executives and two secretaries. In order to accommodate me, we went looking for more office space; we found it in the Swiss Centre in Wardour Street, off Leicester Square, a rather tacky neighborhood. Our offices occupied a floor of a new building that housed the Swiss Tourist Office, various Swiss banks, and the Mövenpick restaurant, an outpost of a chain of excellent Zurich and

Geneva eateries. I felt right at home.

In addition to our international clients, Colin and his team had a longstanding relationship with a number of British outfits. One of these was the British Association of Public Schools. I learned that in Britain "public" actually meant "private". The ruling Labour government had as one of its priorities a policy that would make Britain less class-conscious and elitist. It had brought in a reform system of "comprehensive schools" that were meant to equalize educational opportunities. Inevitably, the privileged classes clung to their traditions, and the controversy over the right direction for the country's education became a hot-button issue, which we were asked to help manage.

Edith and I had made several reconnoitering trips from Geneva to find a place to live. Not knowing where to look in a city with so many options, we were directed by Colin to look at properties in Belgravia, one of London's most upscale neighborhoods. We found a spacious apartment on Eaton Place, in a row of white Georgian houses around the corner from Buckingham Palace. Two adjacent townhouses had been joined to make a spacious floor-through flat. It seemed perfect, and we made a hasty decision to take it. It had beige wall-to-wall carpeting, built-in bookcases and elegant reception rooms. The choice turned out to be quite wrong for us, however. The neighborhood was devoid of shops or street life; it seemed that the other residents only left their swank pads to be ferried somewhere by limousine. Our downstairs neighbor was a single elderly lady, a Marks & Spencer department store heiress. She would leave on the weekends for her country house, leaving the flat in the

hands of the Chinese housekeeper, who used the opportunity to cook for herself and her relatives. Every Sunday
the pungent smell of Chinese cooking came wafting up
into our home. The upstairs neighbor was a wealthy society figure who would sometimes rent a dance floor from
Harrods to entertain his friends right above our bedroom.
The parties lasted well into the night; there was no escaping the throbbing music and thumping of feet. Even when
he did not have company we could clearly hear him walking around; I often would fall asleep only after hearing the
second shoe drop.

After a year in sterile Belgravia, we found a house we
could call home, on Pelham Place, a quiet street in South
Kensington. It was a narrow four-story townhouse and
came with a garage in the back, a rare London commodity.
It was also close to the French Lycée, Jessica's school. I had
actually seen it the year before, while house hunting on
my own. I'd decided it was just the place for us and had
enthusiastically called Edith in Geneva telling her to come
over immediately to see it; but she hadn't been able to get
away, and a day or two later the seller had accepted a bid. A
year later, the original deal had fallen through and the house
was back on the market. This time we did not hesitate. We
made an offer, and the house was ours.

A short time after we were established in our new offices, Hill arrived for his annual visit. Colin Mann arranged
a luncheon to introduce John and me to Enoch Powell, a
colorful and controversial politician. Powell, a Conservative
Member of Parliament and former cabinet minister, had a
huge following among trade unionists as well as middle-class

Tories. He was loudly opposed to unrestricted immigration, and was famous for his "Rivers of Blood" speech predicting that an unfettered influx of foreigners would lead to bloody battles in the streets of London. Colin was an enthusiastic supporter. I must admit that I too was mesmerized by the man's brilliant mind and eloquence, but politically I was turned off by his ideas. I wondered if he saw me as just another unwanted alien. Powell's political philosophy made me cringe: his two other main positions were a strong anti-Americanism and adamant opposition to the government's push to join the European Common Market. His detractors called him a "proto-fascist". Years later, Prime Minister Margaret Thatcher would say of Powell, "He made a valid argument, if in sometimes regrettable terms."

Enoch Powell's anti-American stance stemmed from a suspicion that the United States was out to dismember his beloved British Empire. He became convinced that the U.S.A., in wanting to diminish the power of the British Empire, sought to win world hegemony for itself. He was bitter about having been thwarted in his dream to be appointed Vice-Roy of India, and, later, Governor General of the entire Indian sub-continent. To me, it did not add up: how did Powell reconcile his passion for India with his horror of immigrants from that country?

Immigration, cultural identity and assimilation have long been issues close to my heart. It is personal. After all, I am a serial émigré and expatriate. My own experience has made me a strong believer in the right to freedom of movement. I feel it should be a fundamental human right to live, raise a family, find opportunities and work in a country that is not one's own motherland. Fresh blood brings dynamism to an economy; it is the opposite of stagnation. I recognize, however, that it is a complicated issue. Certainly I was alerted to the downside by some of the anti-immigration prophets I had met: Choppin de Janvry, the French aristocrat who foresaw the turmoil caused by the wave of migrants from the French former colonies; Enoch Powell, the British demagogue who predicted the battles with police in provincial Bradford; and, more recently, Ayaan Hirsi Ali, the Dutch-Somali politician who fled the Netherlands to escape what she defined as "political Islam." I fear the conflicts may grow worse, and that they will not soon be resolved, if ever.

On the same day that we learned that we could close on our purchase of the house on Pelham Place, we had another piece of good news: we had been selected to be the tenants of a country cottage we'd had our eyes on in Oxfordshire. Adjusting to the mores of our environment, we had started to feel the need to escape the city on the weekends. Edith had been searching newspaper ads for country rentals within driving distance of the city, and had explored various suburbs with little success, when one day, driving through the town of Henley-on-Thames, she spied a sign pointing to the hamlet of Nettlebed. It gave her a jolt: she remembered the name from the *Sunday Times* real estate section. She followed the sign and found a charming house for rent in the middle of the village, on the road between Henley-on-Thames and Oxford. The house was quaintly called Apple Tree Cottage. The painters let her in and she immediately fell in love with the place. When she called the property agent, he told her that there were already seven interested parties ahead of her, but if she would send our particulars he would add us to the waiting list. Next we received a call to come to Henley for an interview. We were ushered into the office of a tweedy country gentleman. We found the line of questioning rather bizarre. What were we planning to do with the property? One of the other applicants intended to keep horses. Another wanted to build a swimming pool and formal gardens. Would we be installing a tennis court? No, we said; we liked it just the way it was.

It was never really clear to us why we were the winners, although we did try to speculate. My favorite theory was that it was the Dutch reputation for spotless housekeeping that had given us the advantage. But it was more probably our Belgravia address and my firm's solid financial reputation that swayed the owners. In any case, the cottage was ours, and we lost no time moving in.

Nettlebed was the quintessential English village—a few quaint houses, a pub, an ancient pottery kiln and a post office. The façade of Apple Tree Cottage supported a centuries-old knotted wisteria; there were daffodils, roses climbing the wall, and potted geraniums beside the front door. The back of the garden housed a curiosity left over from World War II: an overgrown air raid shelter. During the war, Ian Fleming, of James Bond fame, had lived in our cottage with his mother. It was part of the Fleming family estate. Peter Fleming, Ian's older brother, was our landlord. He paid us a visit early on to ask whether we had found everything in order; he was a ruddy-faced man and struck us as unpretentious, if a bit reserved. It wasn't until some time later that we learned he had the distinction of being the "Squire" of Nettlebed. He lived at Merrimoles, the nearby Fleming estate. An intrepid traveler, he had written books about his forays into the jungles of Brazil, China, India and Russia. His wife was Celia Johnson, the actress who had starred in the classic British film *Brief Encounter*. As the squire's wife, Celia was given the prerogative of selecting one fourteen-year-old girl from the local school every year to work as apprentice to the mansion's cook or housemaid. We were never invited to Merrimoles, which sounded very grand—it had ten bedrooms, servants' quarters, a pool and a "Casino". We did hear that Evelyn Waugh had declared the place "hideous".

On Sundays the residents of Nettlebed would gather for drinks after church; they took turns hosting this Sunday ritual. It was yet another new custom for us to adapt to. Our next-door neighbors, the Oliphants, were a retired British naval officer and his wife; on the other side lived a spinster, Alice, and her aged mother. Alice was the warden of the local church, painted watercolors and tended a lovely garden. When we asked Alice what to do about an invasion of moles in our front yard, she suggested we should do as she did: pray to the Lord that the vermin would move into the neighbors' yard.

The Flemings never showed up at the Sunday gatherings. We assumed that they moved in more exalted circles. Edith and I couldn't help being made aware of the English class system. Many of our neighbors spoke with a posh Oxford accent that could sound frightfully snobbish. The sherry-before-Sunday-lunch coterie counted among its members the Oliphants; Lord "Jock" Campbell, a sugar magnate who was also, surprisingly, chairman of the left-wing *New Statesman* and who through his friendship with Ian Fleming had founded the literary Booker Prize; and Michael Heseltine, the Tory MP and later Deputy Prime Minster under John Major. Also part of the group were Frits Horn, a fellow Dutch businessman and Sheila, his wife. On the other side of Alice, another friendly couple, Paul and Barbara Irons, lived in an ancient thatched cottage with such low beams that even a man of my height needed to stoop to avoid hitting my head. One Sunday the charming, attractive son of the family was home. He engaged Edith in conversation and told her how difficult it was for a young actor to get a break. Edith told him to keep his chin up, she was sure his big break would come. A month or two later, home for Christmas, he was happy and excited. He had won the lead role in a new musical, *Godspell*. Two decades later we visited Jeremy Irons in his Broadway dressing room, where he had just won a Tony Award for his role in Tom Stoppard's *The Real Thing*, and reminisced about the good old times in Nettlebed.

Next to the Irons lived the youngest couple of the group, Peter and Tracy Poore, who became our closest Nettlebed friends. Peter was the village doctor, Tracy an actress formerly with the Royal Shakespeare Company, and also a playwright. Peter confessed to being envious of our nomadic existence, declaring himself "tired of English village life looking after menopausal women". He and Tracy eventually packed up their three young children and went to live, first, in the Tanzanian jungle and then in Papua New Guinea. Peter wound up becoming the chief medical officer of Save the Children.

Henley-on-Thames was the nearest town, famous for the annual Royal Regatta, the international rowing race. Henley was where we did our weekly grocery shopping. Just outside of town was Henley Management College, where I was asked to give a talk on international public relations. The dean invited us to watch the Regatta from the exclusive Stewards' Enclosure. Having been warned about the dress code—men were required to wear a "lounge suit, blazer and flannels, or evening dress, and a tie," while the women had to wear dresses below the knee, we tried to deck ourselves out accordingly, although we both felt a bit self-conscious. Like at Ascot, most of the women wore wide-brimmed hats; some of the men were in morning coats. We watched the Cambridge and Oxford eights battle it out from a grandstand near the finish line. The champagne flowed freely, the canapés were passed around on silver trays. I was struck by the ostentatiousness of the whole affair, in light of the hard economic times the rest of Britain was going through. One of our fellow guests was the editor of the *Sunday Times*. I asked him *sotto voce* to explain what could justify this extravagance. His answer, in two words: inherited wealth.

The milieu of Pelham Place, a lovely street of white Regency homes, was not dissimilar from "our crowd" in Nettlebed. One of our neighbors was the high-society designer and photographer Cecil Beaton, although he was seldom seen. He lived at Number 8; we were at Number 12. We befriended our neighbors, but remained unreformed aliens. A group of Pelham Place residents occasionally got together for dinner. They were always black tie affairs. When it was our turn to host, we were determined to show our egalitarian roots by breaking one of their traditional rules. After dinner, we suggested that instead of the ladies leaving the gentlemen to enjoy their port and cigars, we all, husbands and wives, should stay together in the same room. No one objected: apparently we were forgiven, being "bloody" foreigners.

Once they discovered we were Dutch, our neighbors accepted us with sympathy, even some fondness. But when, in conversation, they learned that I was working for an American firm and that New York was our home base, they took pity on me. When I countered that I had discovered the merits and advantages of life in America, I was treated with condescension. America was not popular. The view was that America often acted like a bull in a china shop; Americans could be crude and uncivilized. These feelings were not universal, however. The antipathy was at its loudest in response to America's missionary foreign policies. The Vietnam War and the presence of anti-ballistic missiles on British soil were the two issues that drew the strongest resentment.

In the early 1970s, while Washington was in the throes of the Watergate scandal, Britain was going through turbulent times of its own. Inflation had run up to over 20 percent; bombings by the Irish Republican Army created a climate of fear; a coalminers' strike forced the entire country to conserve electricity by instituting a three-day work week. For the privileged, what was happening was just a minor inconvenience. Like our neighbors, I was critical of the Wilson government; in that regard I fit right in.

Fernand and Helga Auberjonois were among our closest friends in London. Helga was the assistant to the editor-in-chief of the Reuters News Agency; Fernand, the son of a famous Swiss painter, was the Pulitzer Prize-nominated dean of American correspondents in London. He had previously worked for *Time* and NBC; now he represented a Midwestern newspaper chain that included *The Toledo Blade* and *The Pittsburg Post-Gazette*. His son René's career on the New York stage was just taking off; we had no idea that he too would become a huge star. Fernand had accomplished several "firsts" as a newspaperman, such as a trip from London to Baghdad using local bus transportation only, and crossing the Khyber Pass on a donkey. One of his pet projects was a book about his King Charles spaniel, *Top Dog*. Helga walked their dog in Kensington Gardens, where it romped with other dogs being exercised by the neighbors' butlers. The Auberjonois spaniel was invited to some very high-class canine birthday parties.

Fernand acted as secretary of The Mid-Atlantic Club of London, a monthly gathering of bankers, business executives, diplomats and journalists interested in the relationships among the United States, Britain and the European Continent, to promote a "free exchange of serious points of view". Walter Lessing, the founder, was an idealistic banker who spoke with a slight German accent. He and Fernand invited me into the club. When I returned to New York in 1974, I joined the sister Mid-Atlantic Club of New York. Its president at the time was the dynamic Zygmunt Nagorski, an expert in international relations who was also program director at the Council on Foreign Relations. I succeeded Zyg as president of the club when Zyg moved to Washington DC.

A conference on the economic relations between the United States and Europe brought me back to Switzerland. The weekend meeting was sponsored by *Fortune Magazine* and took place on the shores of Lac Léman, not far from Geneva. The main speaker, representing a highly personal British point of view, was Denis Healey, the Labour MP and Shadow Foreign Secretary. Healey, a ruddy-faced man with a strong Irish accent, was a vociferous opponent of Britain's closer integration with the Continent. On a bus ride to the conference, he regaled us with bawdy songs and risqué stories. He had built up quite a reputation for his creative turns of phrase, which not infrequently landed him in hot water. Fortunately there were no reporters on the bus. He had us all in stitches.

Five years in London had added another layer to the complexity of my identity. I even adopted a clipped way of speaking. As always, it made me question who I was: an Americanized Dutchman? A Mid-Atlantic gypsy? The proverbial wandering Jew? On the rare occasion that I tried to define myself, I rejected easy clichés such as "cosmopolitan" or "intercontinental", which sounded too much like names of a hotel. Edith and I had not talked about returning to the States. We were perfectly content to remain in Europe, where we were close to our children, our family and friends in Holland and Switzerland, and the places we liked to visit, especially France and Italy.

Then, in early 1974, totally out of the blue, came a call from John Hill telling me to return to New York. Bert Goss had died of Lou Gehrig's disease. Dick Darrow, who had taken over as CEO, had health issues of his own; he was going to need a second cancer operation. Hill retained the position of Chairman, but was getting on in years. He decided that it was time to bolster the senior management team. Hill never expressly stated that I was a candidate to succeed Darrow, but I had my suspicions. Edith accepted our transfer with some reservation. She wasn't looking forward to yet another move, leaving our daughters and our friends behind, and having to settle in somewhere new all over again. She would have to give up a rewarding job at a child guidance clinic in Horsham, on the outskirts of London. The nascent women's movement had come too late for her; it was assumed that as the loyal corporate wife she would pack up and go wherever my job took me. The twins had graduated from university and had started careers in London. Our youngest, Jessica, was applying to college in the UK like her sisters. She did not see why she should follow us to America; she had lived all her life in Europe. Fine, I said, but just to do us a favor, apply to one American college. If you get in, you're coming with us to the States. She applied to Yale. She got in.

We sold our London house and sadly returned the keys of Appletree Cottage to the Flemings. We decided to make the crossing by ocean liner, as we had on our two previous transatlantic moves. We booked ourselves on the last voyage of the legendary *SS France*. As the ship slowly pulled away from the dock at Southampton, we watched a skinny boy run alongside, desperately waving goodbye— Jessica's heartbroken English boyfriend.

It was yet another fresh start. Once again I was on my way to a new home, a new job, a new life; I wondered what my second shot at America would mean for my family and me.

14

///////////////////////////////////////

TO THE TOP AND SIDEWAYS

The New York that awaited us was a different New York than that of our beginnings. Getting used to this New York was easy. It felt like home, and a far more affluent one at that. Two decades earlier, when we'd left for Europe, we had moved out of a modest rented garden apartment in Queens. This time, we were able to afford a sunny, spacious corner co-op on Sutton Place with a dining room, paneled library, maid's room and views of the East River. It was a good time to buy, since the New York real estate market was in a slump. In 1954 I had traveled to work by subway from Queens; in 1974 I was driven to the office in a company limousine. In my starting years at the firm I had worked in a cubicle; now I was entitled to an elegant office on mahogany row, with my personal secretary posted at her desk outside my door. If in England certain aspects of the class system had made me—and especially my wife—uncomfortable, here the trappings of success felt more acceptable. This was, after all, America, a proud meritocracy that rewarded initiative and talent, as opposed to mere accident of birth. Although I did find that New York was a place where class distinctions were neither less strict nor less visible than in tradition-bound Europe, it nevertheless seemed, on the surface at least, far more willing to integrate people with different accents and pedigrees.

One of the first guests to set foot in our new apartment was a childhood friend of mine, Hans Citroen, who worked in the Dutch consulate in New York. In my early teens in Scheveningen, Hans had been one of my crowd, a promising classical pianist. He used to play for us at our parties, alternating with Jaap Feijten, an excellent jazz musician, who was gassed at Sobibor. Hans had worked in the Dutch Resistance before being caught, imprisoned and tortured. After the war it had taken him years to recover from his injuries. Talking about the war with Hans while watching the darkness of the oncoming storm from our as-yet uncurtained windows brought back memories of Jaap and all the other talents lost in the war.

One weekend John Hill invited us to accompany him to his country club, where he kept his horse. The Sleepy Hollow Club, named after *The Legend of Sleepy Hollow* by local resident Washington Irving, was an hour's drive north of the city, close to the Rockefellers' country estate. It was a rich man's playground, and very WASPY. On our second visit we brought our tennis rackets and took a lesson from the club's tennis pro. Hill asked if I was interested in joining the club, as a way of getting out of the city on the weekend. Sure, I said, why not? Hill lined up the required number of sponsors to support my membership application and solemnly informed me that I was only the second Jew to be admitted in the history of the club. I had been preceded just a year or two earlier by the president of Bonwit Teller, the Fifth Avenue fashion store.

This was the second and only other time Hill had ever brought up my Jewish background. The first time had been during one of Hill's annual visits to Europe. We were in Paris, strolling along the Place des Vosges, in the Marais, which happened to be my favorite part of the city: the old Jewish quarter. We passed a synagogue and were surprised to see two armed gendarmes standing guard in front. Apparently they were there to watch for a possible Arab extremist attack. I started talking to Hill about the tribulations of France's Jews during the war. Hill remained silent. Then he said that he disapproved of the power the "Rabbis" had over the Jewish people. This non-sequitur made me realize that he had no clue about Judaism and was not all that informed about the Holocaust either. His lack of interest startled me. I had always assumed Hill wasn't prejudiced; after all, he had hired me. He had also appointed several other Jews to senior positions in the firm, and had close friends like Victor Emanuel, a successful Jewish entrepreneur in the aircraft and appliance industries.

Edith and I were members of Sleepy Hollow for a couple of years, but rarely took advantage of it; it wasn't long before we realized that the country club atmosphere was not for us. We did want to get out of Manhattan on the weekends, however, as we had done in London, and started thinking of finding a country place of our own. We rented a house in Old Greenwich for the summer, which seemed an attractive possibility, but when I took the wrong train home one afternoon and found myself miles away from the station where Edith was waiting to pick me up, I decided the commuter lifestyle was not for me. Our friends Bob and Jeanne Cherneff thought we should come with them one weekend to explore the Berkshires, which they said was their favorite vacation spot. They had plans to retire there. We stayed in a run-down motel in Lee called the Morpheus Arms, and something about the bucolic landscape, the rolling hills, the farms and the quaint towns immediately appealed to us. Several reconnoitering expeditions to the Berkshires later, we were the owners of a piece of land on a glassy lake, with mountain views, in Sheffield. The Gilligans, the family that sold us the land, conveniently had an architect and a builder in their fold; by the next fall the house was ready for us to move in.

My responsibilities at the firm had not changed much. I had been promoted from Vice President to "Vice Chairman International": a rather meaningless distinction. I continued to travel about half the year to Europe and the Far East. In the first couple of years I also visited our eight domestic offices, and attended the monthly meetings of H&K's Board of Directors, which I had joined in 1966. I became marginally more involved with some of our largest national clients, but still spent most of my time managing the overseas operations. My twenty years in Europe had given me a great sense of confidence in my own managerial skills, and if my years in prison camp had taught me anything, it was to be self-reliant. Everything that I knew about PR, management, finance, public speaking and an assortment of other skills,

I had learned on the job, through a mixture of osmosis and chutzpah. When one of our clients, the head of a large international corporation, offered me a highly attractive position in his company, I did not ponder the proposition for long. I was too content being where I was.

The gradual physical disintegration of Bert Goss, picked by Hill to succeed him, had come as a devastating blow to John. Goss had joined the firm toward the end of World War II as the first manager of the Washington office, after a stint as Washington correspondent of *Newsweek*. Hill had brought Goss to New York and had promoted him to President in 1955. Hill and Goss were close friends, but had not always seen eye to eye, especially when it came to Hill's "folly" in selecting me to build the H&K presence in Europe. Goss was cordial with me, but we were never exactly buddies. Early on, I once went to meet Goss and his wife at their hotel in Amsterdam. They were on their way to Paris. When I asked if they were taking the train, Goss, waving his hand, said no, their English-speaking guide would drive them in a limousine. At a time when I was struggling to keep my office afloat, I marveled at the expense of such an indulgence.

Goss had been one of the earliest practitioners of lobbying in Washington, an industry that today employs over forty thousand people. After the war, companies and organizations seeking influence in Washington had had just a handful of law firms to rely on. Hill & Knowlton was possibly the first PR firm to seek support for government policies by mobilizing the "grass-roots" instead of making direct appeals to members of Congress. It had all started with the AIA (Aerospace

Industries Association), the trade organization of American aircraft manufacturers, which retained Hill & Knowlton to resist congressional pressure to defund the Air Force. Post-war public opinion was pushing for a drastic mothballing of expensive aircraft and armaments, which would have dealt a devastating blow to the industry. Hill and Goss helped the client drum up public support for the argument that in an uncertain Cold War future, curtailing the country's air power represented an unacceptable risk.

Another client Goss had been put in charge of was the tobacco industry. During my nineteen years in Europe I was never directly involved in this controversial matter, although I couldn't help being aware of it from the sidelines. It wasn't long before I and many others became convinced that defending smoking against the charges that it could lead to cancer was a losing battle. The Hill & Knowlton executive who worked on the TIRC (Tobacco Industry Research Committee) account fulltime for many years was Tom Hoyt. Tom once confided to me that it was a depressing assignment—in his words, "the cash register never rings," by which he meant that he never received a positive reaction to his efforts. As time went on, it became increasingly clear to Goss and Darrow that the client was not serious about wanting our advice. The TIRC had dug in its heels and was only interested in issuing firm denials. Several attempts to soften the industry position, for example a voluntary health warning on the label of each pack of cigarettes, were rejected. I suspected that one reason for big tobacco's stonewalling was that in the corporate world the legal argument was the one that prevailed: any softening of position increased the chances of costly litigation by tobacco victims. In the face-off between the advisors—the PR men versus the lawyers—the lawyers won out. In our litigious society, the lawyers' arguments may not be without merit, but I have always held that openness should be the preferred route, and will pay dividends in the end. Hill and Goss, frustrated for too long, eventually came around to the same opinion. The firm resigned the account in 1963.

Bert Goss, like many of us, often had to explain that he was not just some highly paid flack. In those days people tended to confuse public relations with publicity, whereas our job was often to devise ways to *avoid* publicity, or at least bad publicity. The only time I ever observed Bert Goss directing a publicity campaign for an individual celebrity was in early 1967. It was an unusual one-shot assignment: Svetlana Stalin, the Soviet dictator's daughter, had been granted asylum in the U.S. days earlier. The office went into overdrive handling innumerable press inquiries and hastily arranging a press conference. The defection of Stalin's favorite daughter was a major news event. Some 400 journalists attended the conference in the Plaza Hotel. It was the largest such gathering since the 1945 announcement of the establishment of the United Nations. *The New York Times* alone devoted five articles to the Svetlana frenzy.

When Bert Goss became incapacitated with ALS, a terrible disease of gradual but inexorable paralysis, it cast a pall over the entire organization, but was especially hard on John Hill. His natural reserve sometimes slipped, revealing a deep anguish at seeing his friend and designated successor die a slow and agonizing death.

Dick Darrow, Goss's successor, was a stout, round-faced, seasoned executive who had joined the company in 1952, one year before me. Dick and Sue, his new bride, had bought an apartment on Sutton Place one block away from ours, so we saw quite a lot of each other. Dick was battling cancer, but that did not stop him from maintaining an active role in the company as well as his many nonprofit board activities. A strong manager and excellent counselor, Dick was the typical Midwestern altruist: he was chairman of his alma mater, Ohio Wesleyan University; Public Relations Chair of the Boy Scouts of America; and, at some point in his career, Mayor of the Town of Scarsdale, NY. He was determined to introduce Edith and me to American football, so on Saturdays he would take us to West Point, where as Advisor to the Academy's Superintendent, he had access to all the games. West Point's Superintendent happened to be Dick's friend General William Westmoreland, the retired commander of the United States military in Vietnam. Dick would usher us into the mess hall to have lunch with the bright-eyed cadets. Afterwards we cheered their team from the grandstand, while Dick tried to explain to us the baffling rules of the game. As Mayor of Scarsdale, Dick had gained fame for calling on the area's segregated country clubs to stop their discriminatory membership policies. He'd had limited success: by the end of the year, one of the exclusive Jewish clubs had accepted one non-English-speaking Chinese millionaire. In his last years, Darrow became a devoted follower of the charismatic preacher Norman Vincent Peale, who officiated at his eleventh-hour wedding to Sue. General Westmoreland also attended, as did Edith and I.

It was Dick Darrow who had originally laid the corner-stone of H&K's expansion throughout Australasia. When Hill sent me to Asia in the 1950s, he sent Darrow to Sydney, where Dick had forged a relationship with Eric White's network in Australia and East Asia. The firm's strong presence and continued success in Hong Kong and South East Asia are Darrow's legacy to the firm—one of his many significant accomplishments.

Hill and Darrow had a mutually mistrusting relationship, however. Many in the firm knew of the tension that existed between them. Hill often mentioned that the "Big I-AM" was detrimental to the company's smooth functioning. It was his way of saying that he didn't like people who had too much ego, a not-so-subtle reference to the CEO he himself had appointed when his chosen successor lay dying. He probably also disapproved of Dick's relationship with Sue, his secretary, while he was still married to his first wife. Darrow confided in me that he wished that Hill, now well into his seventies, would stop coming into the office and constantly looking over his shoulder. Hill was a force to be reckoned with, since he still held the majority of shares in the company he had founded. He never came out and said anything negative about Darrow, but in meetings, his body language would betray his feelings. Once, some years earlier, I was unexpectedly met at the airport on arrival from London by one of my board colleagues. His reason for driving me into town was to ask my help in convincing Hill to step down as chairman. Although I had a reputation as a conciliator, I knew this was an impossible task. Hill, in his own self-effacing manner, made it clear that he wished to remain in control. He identified very strongly with the firm that he had started some fifty years earlier and would continue to personify until his death. There was no way he would agree to take a back seat, let alone stay away from his beloved firm altogether.

In 1974, Rupert Murdoch, until then a media mogul only in his native Australia and Britain, needed advice on breaking into the U.S. market. Darrow and I had dinner with him in New York to discuss how his first United States venture, the supermarket tabloid *Star,* might be positioned to compete with the long successful *National Enquirer.* Murdoch brought along Paul Rigby, his favorite cartoonist. Murdoch was a genial dinner companion, but Darrow and I couldn't compete with Rigby's hilarious stories for Murdoch's attention. Not much was decided. We picked up the check.

Our twin daughters had stayed behind in London, starting their careers. Our youngest, Jessica, was adapting to America and doing well at Yale. Edith went back to study as well: she enrolled at Columbia University for a degree in Gerontology, a rather new and undeveloped field. We joked that her choice of career would come in handy in her husband's old age.

That same year, John Hill suggested that as part of my American education it would be good for me to attend the two-week Aspen Institute Executive Seminar. Aspen's program, based on readings and discussions of the Great Books, in a gorgeous setting high in the Rocky Mountains, proved a rewarding experience. At the end of our stay, I was elected by my group to lead the next year's seminar, so we returned the next summer for another round of inspiring discussions. Our group of twenty leaders in various fields included the Dean of the University of Chicago's Law School, diplomats, a number of senior executives from global companies such as IBM, and two bright young people with engaging personalities who were sponsored by the Mellon Foundation. At breakfast the morning after our arrival, we were seated at a small table with a friendly couple who introduced themselves as the Blackmuns. Only later in the day did we learn of "Harry's" job. He was Supreme Court Justice Harry Blackmun, who had just written the majority decision in the landmark Roe v. Wade case. Another member of the group with whom I hit it off was an obscure judge from the South named Griffin Bell. He kept talking about a man named Jimmy Carter. Those were the days when people were just beginning to ask, "Jimmy Who?" Two years later Griffin Bell became the 72nd Attorney General under President Jimmy Carter. Just before the 1976 election we were houseguests of the Bells in Atlanta. They gave a dinner party for us at which we met several members of Bell's old law firm, some of whom were also to join the Carter Administration. A year later Judge Bell and his wife came and stayed with us in our New York apartment. We enjoyed their company very much, although I did sometimes find his heavy Southern accent hard to understand. Judge Bell had a mischievous streak; he was rumored to have supplied the White House with the spicy Georgian delicacy "rooster pepper sausage," supposedly a bracing aphrodisiac.

I discovered that the American South was another country altogether. Texas ranked high among the weird-

183

est foreign cultures I had ever experienced. It had started when I was still based in Geneva. I received a call from New York telling me to get on the first available flight to Dallas to meet a new client, Jimmy Ling, who needed PR assistance in wooing European investors for his giant LTV conglomerate. In my hotel room I found a note inviting me to dinner at the Lings' home. My taxi turned into a driveway, and as we neared an impressive structure I asked the driver if that was our destination. No, he replied, that's just Mr. Ling's pool cabana. The cab driver also informed me that "Jimmy" was *new money*. The *Murchisons* (oil tycoons of relatively recent vintage themselves), he added in a self-satisfied voice, now that's *old money*. The Ling residence, when it finally came into view, reminded me of Tara in *Gone with the Wind*, especially when I beheld Mrs. Ling, in a long red evening dress, gracefully descending the grand sweep of the staircase. Our firm arranged Ling's tour of the European financial centers, where he successfully raised the money for a new investment target. He later fell on hard times and went bankrupt.

The Ling visit was my introduction to Texas; later we established offices in Dallas and Houston, and for some mysterious reason I was made an honorary citizen of San Antonio. I always enjoyed my visits there: everything was larger than life, and each time I would learn of another quirky Texan law—it was illegal to publish a formula for making beer; a jealous husband was allowed to shoot his adulterous wife; and criminals were to give 24 hours' notice, orally or in writing, to explain the nature of the crime they were about to commit.

We now also had an office in Japan. I was advised that it would strengthen our Japanese office if we would hire a retired Japanese diplomat as the chairman. Ambassador Masao Yagi, a conservative gentleman whose wife always walked a respectful two paces behind him, was amazed when he visited us in the Berkshires and beheld the acreage that was owned by ordinary middle class families, an unthinkable amount of space in Japan's crowded housing market. To me this was just another example of the many cultural gaps separating our nations from one another, causing subtle but serious misunderstandings. It would become a major theme of mine in tackling what was soon to become a major preoccupation: how to change the perceptions on either side of the U.S.–Japan trade imbalance.

In 1975 I was thrown into my first New York-based professional crisis. Our Tokyo office called to tell me that the authorities had come and carted away several boxes of files. Lockheed, the military aircraft manufacturer, was a client; we published the company's Japanese employee publication. It was the height of the Lockheed bribery scandal, which was receiving worldwide media attention. Members of the German, Japanese and Italian governments were being investigated, as was Prince Bernhard of the Netherlands. Our Japanese subsidiary was caught up in the sweep, our links with Lockheed thoroughly investigated. I immediately sent one of my senior associates to Tokyo, but fortunately our files were returned soon afterward; our innocence had been quickly established.

The drama in Tokyo occurred at the time when Dick Darrow lay dying. I made daily trips to Roosevelt Hospital, where Dick was struggling to stay alive. Someone must have told him about the Lockheed situation; in the confused state of mind he was in, that was a mistake. He furiously demanded to be briefed, shouting orders. I had experienced him as a tough and sometimes brusque boss, a hard exterior concealing a gentle heart. Now all I saw was an angry, frustrated, sick man raging against approaching death.

Darrow's death, in March 1976, hit me hard. My mother had died of the same disease not long before. Both had struggled with cancer. Both had suffered. What was this illness, what caused it? I was moved to become more informed about it, and this led me to Richard Rivlin, a New York internist and researcher at Memorial Sloan Kettering Cancer Center, who had begun studying the relationship between nutrition and cancer. He asked me to chair his nutrition research committee, to help raise money for internships at the cancer hospital. Awareness of the role of diet in many illnesses, including cancer, was just starting to get off the ground. Rivlin was a pioneer in the field, and was also trying to introduce healthful menus for the patients at New York Hospital, across the street from Sloan Kettering. We interviewed a number of young physicians slated to be trained on Rivlin's team. Some came from as far away as Japan and Israel; they helped to spread the word around the world about nutrition as a major health factor.

Hill was still coming to the office, although he had ostensibly retired. He had proposed to the board that the function of CEO should be shared by Bill Durbin and me. Bill took the title of Chairman; I became President. Besides Bill and me, our new board was composed of our longtime

CFO Charlie Puzzo and six other senior department heads. Bill and I had adjacent offices. Our relationship was a rare one; we were truly interchangeable. Bill, who at 59 was my senior by seven years, had joined the firm after a career in the FBI and the pharmaceutical industry. I had first met Bill when he was still a client, the in-house PR director of American Cyanamid, my first multinational client in Geneva; he had joined H&K not long afterward. We had always had a very good working relationship, and had become personal friends over the years. Prior to my move to New York, on the rare occasion when I didn't stay with the Hills on Park Avenue, I would go to the Durbins in New Jersey, where, in an atmosphere of devout Catholicism, I was warmly received. I must confess that I found it rather disconcerting to open my eyes in the guest room in the morning to be confronted with images of Jesus on the cross. I never quite understood how Bill reconciled his religious devotion with his need for alcohol. However, Bill always functioned well, even after his usual multi-martini lunch. He was a true extrovert with a sweet temperament. He inspired loyalty from the staff members who worked closely with him; they adored him.

Like Darrow and Goss, Hill also wrestled near the end. He remained a staunch individualist in full command of his faculties into advanced age, until a brain tumor destroyed him. His facial expression did not change; a pair of intelligent eyes sparkled behind his rimless glasses, his keen intellect cloaked in modesty. When he got fed up with the hospital, he simply walked out. But when, in 1977, he at last gave up the fight, I felt a deep sense of loss for the man who had been such a close friend and mentor. At the memorial service in Lincoln Center's Alice Tully Hall, attended by a sizable crowd, I told the assembly that Hill had not been given enough credit for having pioneered a number of important innovations that are now standard in the industry. These included the first Washington operations; crisis management; an education department for the preparation and dissemination of materials to be used in schools; TV and radio training for industry spokesmen; financial PR, such as shareholder communication and investment community relations; and an environmental department to advise clients on air and water pollution, or similar issues. Throughout his years at the helm, he had always exemplified a strong sense of ethics, and imposed his principled standards on the entire organization.

It was also a moment to reflect what it was that Hill had seen in me. When we first met in his New York office, all I'd had to offer was some limited writing experience, a history of survival based on luck and tenacity, and the gumption to talk my way into a job by professing a desire to bring public relations back to Europe. His friends always said he had a great sense of intuition; in my case, it can only have been instinct that prompted him to take a chance on this callow young man. I was always amazed at the faith he had in me, even when we were nearly fired by our first and only client in Geneva, or during the seven lean years of European losses. Finally, his decision to call me back to New York as a candidate to lead the firm had been a gutsy move. Although I always tried to ignore the office gossip, I did find out later that he had had to justify appointing a foreigner, a Jew no less, to run the show. At the time, I did not give it much thought; it did not strike me as all that extraordinary that I was one of just a handful of non-U.S. citizens heading up one of the original "white shoe" U.S. consultancy firms. Hill was convinced, as always, that he knew what he was doing. I just felt privileged to have been taken under his wing.

Several months after Hill's death, I received a call from the Chancellor of Indiana University, Herman Wells, asking to see me about a matter concerning John's will. Wells, an impressive figure in the world of higher education and one of John's beloved Hoosiers, spent over an hour in my office explaining that Hill had bequeathed a considerable sum of money to the university. Over the years the two friends had decided that I.U.'s famous music school and a school of journalism should be the main beneficiaries of Hill's generous bequest. Unfortunately however, this detail was never put into writing. Wells asked me to convey to Elena, with his regrets, that there would be no John Hill School of Journalism or any other building named after him; when the Indiana lawmakers heard about Hill's gift, they conveniently reduced the state's financial support to the university by a sum equal to that left in John Hill's will. It was another of life's cautionary tales: I could just imagine John turning over in his grave at the news that his legacy had gone into installing culverts and repairing toilets.

15

//

A HIGH-FLYING DUTCHMAN

I threw myself into the role of CEO, determined to build on Hill's legacy while keeping the firm on a sound financial footing in the dicey economy of the 1970s. There was no reliable precedent to follow on how best to manage a consulting firm. Our company, like our main competitors, had always been run by professionals who were experts in their counseling fields, but were not necessarily trained administrators. PR pro meant just that: consult with the client, analyze the problem, give sound advice, and the rest would take care of itself. For Hill and other pioneers like Harold Burson, whose firm Burson-Marsteller became our main competitor, interacting with clients—studying problems and recommending solutions—remained the mainstay of daily activities. Running the company was a secondary concern. If they were lucky, they secured the services of an experienced financial wizard to head the accounting department (later bombastically named chief financial officer). As early as the 1950s, Hill had had the foresight to engage Price

Waterhouse, then the most prestigious accounting firm in the country, to devise an effective, profitable and fair method of client billing. The formula they came up with mirrored our own accountants' system: charging the client on the basis of hours spent on the client's behalf. H&K was the first firm in its field to introduce the "time sheet", a discipline imposed on the entire organization from the top down; everyone, from the chairman to the youngest trainee, was expected to keep these records. When the study was completed, Hill promptly hired Harry Cooper, the Price Waterhouse man who had helped to set up our system, and put him in charge of our firm's finances. In managing the internal aspects of the company business, i.e. finance, accounting, human resources, real estate, insurance, pension plans and benefits, etc., the buck was passed down from above. Management did not concern itself overly much with running its own affair. There was also no systematic PR for our PR firm; the cobbler's children were forced to go without shoes. We do not need to go grubbing after new business, John Hill had proclaimed. Clients in need of our services will know how to find us. It sounded arrogant, but it worked.

In time, however, adaptations were made. As the firm grew, the administrative functions became more complicated. We were constantly faced with new management issues, and had to learn how to handle them as they came up, haphazardly or by osmosis. In time, I'm told, I became a "bloody good administrator".[10]

In the mid-1970s a Harvard Business School study found

10 In the words of Eric White, our Australian associate and board member, in a confidential letter to Charlie Puzzo discussing the post-Darrow succession.

that Hill & Knowlton's clients represented ten percent of the country's total economy. We preferred to use another yardstick: our firm was retained by one half of Fortune Magazine's 100 largest American corporations. The challenge was to maintain the quality, forward momentum and creativity required to keep our rank as the world's largest PR firm. When Bill Durbin and I divided up the responsibilities between us, my years abroad made me the logical choice for overseeing international operations, which now included 22 offices around the world. It also meant that I continued my role as chief collector of our overdue fees from the foreign potentates who were our clients.

My first exposure to that role went all the way back to the 1950s, when I was based in Paris. I had received a call from New York instructing me to go to the Hotel Georges V to meet with President Tubman of Liberia. I was told to make sure I brought a briefcase. In the presidential suite, Tubman, a courteous, cigar-puffing gentleman, engaged me in small talk. After a suitable interval, he solemnly handed me several manila envelopes containing $10,000 in cash: fees for past service. Feeling like a character in a film, I scurried to the Citibank office on the Champs Elysées with my bursting briefcase, and hurriedly deposited the money in a safe deposit box. Our work for Liberia was to obtain press coverage for Tubman's visit to Washington. One thing we tried not to publicize was that when Tubman was home in Monrovia, the capital was occasionally plunged into darkness; it was widely known that that meant that the President was visiting his mistress in town. The electricity was shut off to conceal his comings and goings.

In the 1970s the Kingdom of Morocco retained us to help it persuade American companies to set up manufacturing plants on its soil. It was a troubled relationship. We were having a hard time obtaining sufficient background materials for our publicity mill, and our bills were long overdue. So I packed my bags and flew to Rabat, where His Majesty King Hassan II and his chief of staff received me on a terrace of the royal palace with sweeping views of the city. After I had explained our need for more information and facts, the King impatiently ordered his counselor to take care of it at once. Next I broached the delicate subject of our unpaid bills. Again the King displayed his displeasure; not with us, but with his own underlings. Then he graciously invited me to attend the wedding of the daughter of his kinsman, the Moroccan Ambassador to Washington, who, the King explained, had not been able to attend our meeting on account of the upcoming nuptials in Marrakesh. The counselor took copious notes, agreed to arrange for me to be flown to Marrakesh, then walked me out with the assurance that everything would be taken care of immediately.

The lavish wedding ceremony took place in the gardens of a beautiful villa in an imposing compound. I remember a chorus of black-robed women bewailing the loss of a beloved virgin. The festivities were to last several days, and the King was expected to put in an appearance at some point, but after the first day's dinner—featuring an astoundingly delicious pigeon pie—I flew back to New York empty-handed. We waited for some sign that payment was on its way; none was forthcoming. By the time it finally materialized, we had resigned the account.

The Indonesians were slow payers too. A consortium of three New York investment banks retained by the Indonesian government had recommended our firm. We were to assist in the effort to attract American investment. Indonesia had long depended on its oil wealth, but now it was ready to diversify. It wanted to present itself as an attractive location for a whole range of industries. Like other dictators, President Suharto relied on the military to run the country, but had surrounded himself with a smart economic team as well. The two ministers we reported to had been educated in the U.S. and were known as the "Berkeley Mafia." They were part of a group of economic advisors led by Professor Widjojo, the Coordinating Minister for Economy, Finance and Industry. The first time I met the Professor, he looked at my calling card and asked point blank whether there was a Dutch family connection. When I told him that I was in fact Dutch, he embraced me and said how pleased he was that we could communicate in a language he was more fluent in than English. By the 1970s the Dutch-Indonesian conflict had begun to fade, and, fortunately for me, friendly relations were being restored.

I made several visits to Jakarta, and the sticky atmosphere always brought me back to my turbulent teen years. I had a vivid memory of a hike in the hills of Western Java, when I'd come face to face with a large, hissing cobra snake, which our intrepid Javanese guide had speared without batting an eyelid. Jakarta was more crowded now, but the Javanese women still washed the laundry in the dirty river, and the streets were clogged with tens of thousands of bicycles, a lasting legacy of the Dutch colonials.

Eventually the monies we were owed for our work for the government were so long overdue that we threatened to walk away from the account. Our pleas and threats were ignored. One fine day Gavin Anderson, a young Australian I had hired in London and who had followed me to New York, reported that he had solved the problem. He had woken up one of the ministers in the middle of the night, Indonesia time, and said that he would keep calling every night until payment was received. A bank transfer arrived a few days later.

I remained Hill & Knowlton's point man in dealing with Japanese issues. It seemed that I just could not escape my past. My abiding interest in Japan led me to join New York's Japan Society, where I sat on a panel with the media star David Halberstam to discuss the future of U.S.–Japan relations. This was a time when the Japan–U.S. trade imbalance was making headlines; there was widespread fear that Japan would crush the American economy with its cheap imports. I also became a member of the Japan–U.S. Business Council, an organization of senior business executives, consultants, lawyers and accountants from both countries that met to exchange views on sensitive issues such as bilateral tariffs, investments, and import/export. It was assumed that each side would brief and counsel its respective government. I suspect that in the case of Japan that may have been the case; as for our influence on Washington, I doubt that any attention was paid.

A combination of arrogance and self-righteousness on the part of the Japanese occasionally shone through the veneer of cordiality. At a meeting in Minneapolis, the Japanese president of the Council revealed his true view of U.S.-Japanese business relations. He proclaimed belligerently that the Americans could carry on with the excellent job they were doing in marketing the goods the Japanese produced for them. The next day's unofficial apology blamed the tone and content of the president's speech on the fact that he'd had rather too much to drink.

It was a strange and heady experience for me, to find myself in the position of wagging my finger at Japanese business leaders, many of whom had surely tried to stamp out the likes of me thirty years before. Surrounded by Japanese executives at a Business Council dinner, I was suddenly brought back to the times in the jungle when, starving, I was forced to watch the Japanese guards enjoying a copious meal. We had been convinced they were eating the Red Cross rations we were supposed to receive and which never materialized. My Japanese colleagues' hearty appetites also triggered painful memories of our pitiful treks to the camp's kitchen—two large black cooking pots, one filled with a watery soup with a few strings of green floating in it, the other with rice, that was sparingly strewn into the soup. It was our only meal of the day. We all hungered for the blackened crust of rice left at the bottom of the pot, but only the lucky few who still had the strength to shoulder their way to the front were able to make off with the precious scrapings.

In dealing with the Japanese, I sometimes wondered how we had won the war. I knew that we had trounced the enemy in the end. But in terms of sheer cunning, I felt the Japanese could outsmart the Americans any day. This was a time when I still viewed the disagreements between Japan and America from a myopic European perspective. That is not to say that I did not share the American indignation about Japan's stubbornness in maintaining high tariffs on agricultural products and manipulating the value of the yen to its competitive advantage. It was a period of over-wrought American fear of being demoted to number two in the ranking of the most powerful economies of the world. When Japanese interests bought golf courses, a Hollywood film company, and, most alarming of all, Rockefeller Center, in the very heart of New York City, the media went into a frenzy. In reality, there was never any real danger of Japan overtaking the U.S. As in so many other instances, the issue had a relatively short shelf life. Japan's bubble burst in the early 1990s, plunging the country into a recession from which it has not yet completely recovered.

Within the broad range of issues that concerned me, Japan always retained a place near the center of my thinking. In a speech in Hakone at the plenary opening session of the Japan-U.S. Business Council, I used the term "culture gap," which did not yet have the currency it has today. It caught the attention of the business press in the U.S., the Netherlands, and Japan. Over time I had become convinced that the distance between our two cultures was much wider than that separating us from China or the Indian subcontinent. I was always struck by the differences; for example, the organizational skills the Japanese possessed made a big impression on me, and their attention to the most minute details. On the bus ride from Tokyo to Hakone, two contingents of conferees arriving in the pouring rain were met by the exact same number of hotel employees, each holding aloft an umbrella. It was a scene straight out of *Les Parapluies de Cherbourg*. I gave many a talk about bridging this "culture" or "communication gap" between our two countries. A study we conducted showed that, whereas Japanese businesses sent Japanese employees who were experts on all things American to the U.S., their American counterparts relied on hiring local Japanese staff. The few Americans that were sent to Tokyo were hired for their business skills, not their Japanese language proficiency or familiarity with the culture. We found that our American clients did not turn to Japanese Studies departments to recruit new talent—a definite disadvantage when it came to conducting business in Japan.

To this day I am puzzled by the complete turnaround of Japanese public opinion after Japan's 1945 surrender. After adhering to a dogma of racial hatred of the Caucasian enemy during the war, they turned slavishly obedient toward the U.S. occupying forces as soon as it was over, and immediately expressed exaggerated admiration for General MacArthur. How a populace prepared to commit mass suicide for its country (as in Okinawa) could change so quickly into an obediently bowing, reborn nation, going from the euphoria of the victor to the despondency of the victim, is a phenomenon for which I have never found a rational explanation.

The "Culture Gap" was second cousin to "The Clash of Civilizations," a controversial theory propounded by the conservative social scientist Samuel Huntington of Harvard University. As president of the Mid-Atlantic Club of New York, I once had occasion to introduce Professor Huntington as our luncheon speaker, and had an interesting chat with him afterwards. Huntington was roundly attacked for his premise that future conflicts between civilizations were inevitable. He had built a complicated construct of the world's nations into a new world order, arbitrarily putting some into camps to which I did not think they belonged. From his broad canvas, the only terrain where clashes looked to me to be unavoidable was the Muslim versus the Western world. Twenty-five years later, I wonder whether Huntington's harshest critics should at least reconsider. Another speaker at the monthly Mid-Atlantic Club luncheon in the Whist Club, an old brownstone on the New York's Upper East Side, was Benjamin Netanyahu, then Israeli Ambassador to the U.N. The future Prime Minister's talk centered on Israel's security needs in the light of the Arab threat. We had our own little security crisis when the Ambassador and his bodyguard suddenly disappeared into thin air. To our relief they had just sneaked down the servants' back staircase to find an empty men's room.

Another part of the world requiring my attention was Africa. Our firm's connection with that continent seemed almost always to involve work to gain Washington recognition, not so much for the country itself as for its vainglorious leader. Thirty years after my interaction with President Tubman of Liberia, I had occasion to meet another African leader, President Bongo of Gabon. Accompanied by two senior associates, I flew to Libreville, where our first appointment was a dinner in the home of Prime Minister Léon Mébiame. One entered his residence via a long tunnel that served as an art gallery featuring an extensive collection of museum-quality carvings by artists from

Gabon and neighboring states. The next night we were the guests of the U.S. Ambassador, a jolly old Africa hand who regaled us by snatching a sword from the wall behind him and slashing the neck of the excellent Bordeaux he served. The Ambassador informed us that President Bongo's aim was to curtail his country's dependence on France and enter into a more lucrative relationship with America. Asked to wait in an anteroom before our audience with the president the next day, we were confronted by his security detail: a half dozen grim Algerians armed with machine guns. The president, it seemed, chose to be guarded by well-paid foreign mercenaries rather than his own subjects, who were perhaps rather less reliably loyal. From his throne-like chair on an elevated platform, the president expressed his disappointment and frustration: why had he not yet received an invitation from the White House for an official visit? I explained that there were hundreds of nations represented in Washington; the waiting list was long and required patience. It was the wrong answer. What followed was a long and angry tirade vaunting Gabon's strategic geographical position and its offshore oil reserves. Gabon is very important to America, Bongo thundered, and it is in America's interest to woo Gabon away from France. But with French troops guarding the regime against possible uprisings, the French national oil company holding long-term contracts, the French educational system firmly in place and, above all, successive French governments firmly believing in the mission of imposing their civilization and language on their former colonies, France was unlikely to relinquish its hold. The president went on to trumpet his democratic record as evidence of his great affinity with America, although he failed to mention that in the national elections he always won by a questionable 99% of the vote. We were unable to arrange a presidential visit to Washington, and gave up the account. Some years later, in 2003, the lobbyist Jack Abramoff offered to do the arranging for an alleged $9 million fee. Bongo met with President George W. Bush ten months later, in May 2004, although there was never any official acknowledgement of the Abramoff transaction. Ali Bongo, who succeeded his father as president-for-life, was received by President Obama in 2011.

The trip to Gabon provided me with an opportunity to visit the jungle home of the late Albert Schweitzer, a hero of mine. We chartered a one-engine plane to fly us to Lambarene, where the good doctor, theologian, philosopher, medical missionary, Nobel Peace Prize winner and devotee of Bach organ music had founded a hospital deep in the jungle along the Ogooue River. The Governor of the province gave us a ceremonious welcome; a children's choir serenaded us in French patois. Schweitzer's housekeeper showed us around the premises. Schweitzer's beloved organ was still there, a startling sight in the tropical rain forest.

Next on the list of governments who came to us for help in attracting foreign investment was Saudi Arabia. The Saudi government wanted to explore investment alternatives to oil. The Saudis, wealthy beyond imagination, were thinking of the far-off day when alternative sources of energy might nibble away at their vast income. We sent a staff member to Riyadh, but the relationship did not last long. In New

York, the Saudi Ambassador to the U.N., a Jordanian by birth, began to demand that we help him draft fulminating anti-Israel speeches. When he grew increasingly adamant, refusing to acknowledge that this was political work, and thus not part of our agreement with his government, we resigned the account rather abruptly.

John Hill had laid down the law: Hill & Knowlton would not be caught up in political issues, whether domestic or foreign. Under my leadership we held to that rule. The work we did for the governments of Indonesia and Morocco passed the test because it served only the countries' economic interests. France was another nation that retained us in order to attract U.S. investment. In the case of Liberia and Gabon, we found ourselves catering to the personal vanity of the ruler, and strove not to get embroiled in the politics. We dealt with the tariff issue for Hong Kong, and after a devastating earthquake, Mexico turned to us for assistance in boosting the tourism industry. For a long time we likewise helped the Bahamas with its tourism promotion, but we lost the account when our account executive made a pass at the pretty wife of a senior government official.

On my watch, I frequently had to respond to pressure from Wall Street bankers who wanted us to counsel various governments or leaders who were on the receiving end of bad press. Among the potential clients I found myself turning down were President Salazar of Portugal, President Marcos of the Philippines, South Africa's Apartheid regime, and the Greek military junta. Our refusal was always cloaked in non-ideological pragmatism: we could not take on the account, I would explain, because although there might be some among our clients or employees who sympathized with the prospective client's policies and practices, there would invariably be others who would disapprove and protest. As a company representing many different constituencies, we had to remain neutral. We also explained that if correspondents in Lisbon, Johannesburg, Manila or Athens wrote articles in *The New York Times* about the ugly repression they were witnessing, there was nothing we could do to alter the facts. These governments were not exactly models of democracy. I was sorry when H&K's longstanding policy of staying out of politics and away from suspect regimes was set aside after my retirement. Good for the bottom line, certainly, but not for the firm's reputation.

John Hill loved to say, "This business keeps you young." I was used to the ever-changing nature of the profession itself, and was conscious of having to adapt our business practices accordingly. Issue response, crisis management, satellite communications, the changing technology of the workplace, the home computing revolution, the growth of the multinationals, an increasingly vocal public, a well-organized environmental movement, increasing global interdependence—all these came with new challenges or problems that landed on my desk every day.

Our firm was recognized for the quality of its durable staff and our long-term relationships with clients. Some clients stayed for decades; senior staff turnover was minimal, especially when compared to others in the field. Our policy of telling the client not what he wanted to hear but what we honestly thought was the best course of action, paid off in spades in client loyalty. The client might not take our unwelcome advice, but could be counted on to return for more of the same, sometimes even with a reluctant, "You were right."

One day I received a call from the Chairman of Pillsbury. Could I come to Minneapolis to discuss an important matter? When I met him in his office, he confided that morale in the company's headquarters was low. The assignment was to conduct a survey and come up with recommendations on how to improve the employees' team spirit. When the survey was completed, I flew back to Minneapolis to inform him of the results. We met in private. So, he asked me, what did you come up with? "The problem is *you*," I told him bluntly. When he asked for specifics, I said that according to the report he rarely left the executive floor and had very little contact with the rest of the staff. He grunted, then asked me to leave him one copy of the report. He requested that all other copies be destroyed.

As President of Hill & Knowlton, overseeing a staff of 1,300, I found myself frequently juggling to keep the firm's competing departments in harmony. These fiefdoms, which I called "baronies", were headed up by very capable executives. Each of them was possessed of a healthy competitive streak, and enough ego to feel he would be just as capable of leading the firm as this foreign interloper. I didn't mind. In spite of these undercurrents, I had a very solid relationship with each of them individually.

Dick Cheney (no relation to the former Vice President) and Bob Gray were two colleagues who made significant contributions to our success. Both were generally much better known than the foreigner who was now their boss. My first encounter with Cheney was in the early 1960s. On a visit from Europe, walking by an office on our executive floor, I spied through an open doorway a figure standing on his head. This was Dick Cheney, yoga devotee and one of the best croissant bakers in America. Dick was the head of our financial relations department, and was admired for his frankness. He told one client CEO to stop drinking and another to stop flaunting his affair with an ambitious employee. In the 1980s, based on Dick's stellar reputation, our financial department became involved in many a bitter corporate takeover battle. Dick preferred to be on the side of the underdog—i.e. the company that was on the defensive. His yoga may have been a necessary way to relieve the stress. No one in the firm knew that Dick had a secret life: he was studying to become a psychoanalyst. To everyone's surprise, he established a successful practice after he retired.

Bob Gray was the ultimate Washington insider. Early in his career Gray had been Secretary of the Eisenhower Cabinet. He had also been on the Committee to Elect Richard Nixon. John Hill was always fond of visiting the capital, where as a guest at Bob Gray's legendary dinner parties he could count on hobnobbing with the town's elite. I too appreciated the chance to mingle with Washington's movers and shakers at his house. I met an Associate Justice of the Supreme Court, the Postmaster General, the Comptroller of the Currency and an assortment of senators, congressmen and widely known Washington journalists. Gray, a bachelor, was a charmer who was known for squiring various ladies about town, including Nixon's secretary Rosemary Woods. Many people in the office were convinced Gray was behind

Rosemary Woods' "accidental" missing 18-minute mishap with the Nixon White House tapes.

1982 marked 200 years of unbroken diplomatic U.S.– Netherlands relations, a milestone that was celebrated in the Netherlands with a conference hosted by Queen Beatrix. It was decided that something should be done to reciprocate here in the U.S. as well. I was asked to serve as Vice-Chairman of the Netherlands Bicentennial Committee. One of the highlights of the events we organized in September 1983 was a cocktail party hosted by Vice President George H.W. Bush at his residence. There was also a dinner at the State Department and a visit to the boardroom of the Federal Reserve, where Chairman Paul Volcker excused himself early on, saying he had pressing matters to attend to, and insisted that I take his chair. Washington D.C.—what a place for fantasies.

My extracurricular activities were varied; I was asked to sit on a number of nonprofit boards, including chairing the International Advisory Council of New York's International Center. The New York Legal Aid Society proved one of the toughest boards I ever served on. I joined that board at the same time as Bill Bernbach, the creative director who had come up with the *Think Small* campaign for Volkswagen and created the man with the eye patch for Van Heusen shirts. Bill and I were the only non-lawyers in a roomful of lawyers, each of whom considered himself an expert on publicity and PR. I learned just how true the old saying was: put twenty lawyers together in one room and you'll get twenty different opinions. After spending some time with this legal cabal, I was made a member of the Executive Committee, which conducted business in a much calmer atmosphere.

It was an era of corporate takeovers and acquisitions. John Hill had at various times entertained the notion of taking the company public, but in considering the pros and cons, the cons had always outnumbered the pros. In 1972, Prentice-Hall had shown interest in acquiring H&K, but it never went anywhere. Ten years later however, a decade when the major advertising agencies were actively looking to expand, we found ourselves being courted simultaneously by J. Walter Thompson and Ogilvy & Mather. I did not solicit these approaches, although I had considered the idea, as a way of accessing the capital we needed for further expansion.

Bill Durbin, Charlie Puzzo and I decided to enter into discussion with our two suitors. All parties tried to keep the negotiations completely secret. On a personal level, I got on well with J. Walter Thompson's CEO, Don Johnston, a gracious, affable man. One of JWT's attributes that I found very attractive was that, like our firm, Thompson had several very longstanding and loyal clients, including the Ford Motor Company. I also enjoyed becoming acquainted with David Ogilvy, an icon of the advertising industry. One early morning meeting with the Ogilvy top brass took place in our Sutton Place apartment. Edith tiptoed in from the kitchen to serve breakfast to our guests. Since the only way out of the kitchen was through the dining room, Edith, not wanting to disturb us, waited patiently in the kitchen for a couple of hours until the visitors had left.

In July 1980 the announcement was made: Hill & Knowlton was to be acquired by the Thompson agency.

To accommodate the addition of H&K's 1,300-plus staff and its long list of prestigious clients, the board of J. Walter Thompson decided to create a holding company. Called the JWT Group, it encompassed the old advertising firm, our company, and a number of smaller units. I was asked to join the board. The marriage between the largest advertising agency and the biggest PR firm was a newsworthy event: it made the front page of *The New York Times*. One of my associates described me in the article as "unflappable." Little did he know my true state of mind. A week before signing the merger documents, I had been in Sicily attending a management conference of our European team when I'd received a call from our lawyer. One of my colleagues on the H&K board was going to abstain. I had counted on a unanimous vote. I was shattered, but, sworn to secrecy, could not talk it over with any of the others present. Skipping the rest of the day's conference, I took a taxi from the hotel where our meeting was being held and drove to Syracuse. Walking through the ancient Greek and Roman ruins for two hours helped to restore my equilibrium.

It was Bob Gray, our man in Washington, who had changed his mind and withheld his vote. It later turned out that Gray had been hoping to raise enough funds to take over the company himself. As it was, I received a surprise call from President-elect Ronald Reagan in November 1980, before the JWT deal was finalized. Would I mind very much, he drawled in his charming voice, if he borrowed Bob Gray for a while so that Gray could help with the Presidential Inauguration? Of course, I stammered; with pleasure. So Gray took a leave of absence to become

Co-Chairman of the Inauguration Committee. He never returned, however. After organizing the glittering Reagan Inaugural festivities, Bob quit and started his own company, the lobbying firm Gray and Company. He took it public some five years later. Soon after my retirement, however, Gray returned to the fold, selling the majority interest in Gray and Company back to H&K in 1987 and taking the title of Worldwide Chairman.[11]

I am often asked what my relationship with Bob Gray was like. Professional frictions aside, I got on well with him, and he seemed to like me, although it was hard to tell, since Bob was the ultimate charmer who was everyone's friend. Bob was a true courtier, always ready with the right gesture, compliment or gift. When early in my tenure I invited our senior management group to our modest weekend house in the Berkshires, Bob flew in on a private plane. He brought Edith a Hermès scarf that she cherished many years after. Once he was his own boss and no longer bound by our rules, he took on clients John Hill would have frowned on, including Haiti under Baby Doc and China after Tiananmen Square, earning him the moniker of the "Darth Vader of Lobbyists"[12]. His desertion harmed our Washington office considerably, since he took quite a number of clients with him; what I

---

11 It is important for me to set the record straight and point out that none of Gray's controversial clients that were mentioned in his obituaries in the *NY Times* and *Washington Post* in 2014 (i.e. Kuwait, Haiti, Angola, the RNC, Rev. Sun Myung Moon and the Church of Scientology) were served on my watch.

12 Susan B. Trento, *The Power House: Robert Keith Gray and the Selling of Access and Influence in Washington,* St. Martin's Press 1992

found harder to forgive was that in taking on bad actors as clients, he had not done our profession's reputation any favor.

Bill Durbin retired after the purchase by JWT Group was completed. He and his wife moved to Arizona, where within a year he was felled by liver disease. After his departure I was named Chairman, President and CEO by the JWT board. The new titles did not change my routine, except that I now also participated in the monthly board meetings of JWT. At those meetings the various sectors of the Group reported on their monthly financials and any new developments. It gave me some insight into the art of advertising; some of the advertising presentations I witnessed were brilliant, some rather unimpressive, and a few wretchedly boring.

Other than Gray's defection, the transition from running an independent company to becoming part of a publicly traded one went smoothly. I retained complete autonomy over our operation. I never felt any pressure to adjust our policies. Although there were internal pressures, with certain segments of the H&K organization not coming up to my expectations—some foreign offices, such as Dublin and Tokyo, were always struggling—I never had to justify my actions to the board. I felt Don Johnston had my back. From my experience with mergers and acquisitions I knew that we were in the honeymoon phase and that we might have to deal with shareholder pressure somewhere down the line; but for now, the going was smooth—almost *too* smooth. There were plenty of fresh challenges ahead, of course: broadening our entrée into South America, opening up Eastern Europe, modernizing our administration through the use of new technologies. All groundbreaking ventures, but it wasn't until we began to explore China that I was gripped by the old sense of excitement at being involved in something completely new.

At the suggestion of our Hong Kong management team, which had conducted the preliminary research, I flew to Beijing for the opening of our first Chinese mainland office. We had hired a young Canadian journalist who was married to a Chinese woman and was fluent in Mandarin. Walking with our Canadian manager through the city one Sunday, I saw that he attracted quite a bit of attention: a tall, blond Westerner with a Chinese toddler on his shoulder. The rest of the staff consisted of one secretary and the driver of the company car, which we rented through a governmental trade agency. We soon discovered that our chauffeur was a government spy who reported back to headquarters on everything that went on in our office. This being China, we had to live with it: that was the price one paid doing business there. I returned to China a couple of years later for the official opening of our second office in Shanghai, which was celebrated with an elaborate Chinese banquet. Mindful of my experience in Hong Kong two decades earlier, I had become adept at pretending to empty my glass when the rounds of toasts began.

In 1984, having been in New York for ten years, I decided it was time for me to become a United States citizen. To become a naturalized American, I would have to give up my Dutch citizenship, which I had been reluctant to part with. (This was before the Dutch government changed its policy to permit dual nationality.) As a Netherlands national, member of the European Union, I felt I was a citizen of a wider world. Would becoming an American shrink my horizons? I had never felt any pressure from colleagues to change my nationality for the sake of the firm. Foreign CEOs of American organizations were rare but not unheard of. No, in the end, the decision was prompted by a more banal reason: the rigmarole I was put through when I visited Grumman, an important Long Island–based client. As a foreign national, getting in to see the defense contractor involved reams of frustrating red tape, causing some raised eyebrows. It was time to throw in the towel; I accepted the fact that my roaming days were over. America was my home now. On a bright January day I was sworn in by Judge Shirley Kram on board the decommissioned *U.S.S. Intrepid* on the West Side of Manhattan, with a view of the Statue of Liberty in the distance.

16

///////////////////////////////////

THE GOOD LIFE

Our extended family was vacationing in the Canary Islands, a Spanish territory off the West Coast of Africa. It was December 1985, the Christmas holidays. The warm sunshine and sea air made us all very healthy and energetic. The place we had rented had no telephone connection. Each morning I would walk over to the post office to place a call to the office to check in. I'd wait in line for the postmistress to write down the telephone number; since there was no direct cable under the ocean, my call had to go by way of Madrid. It took at least an hour for the connection to be made. When I finally got through, I'd ask what was going on. Every day the response was the same: my secretary told me that no, there were no messages for me, and no crises to report. When I asked her to transfer me to one of my associates, none was available, or they were too busy to take my call. Obviously they wanted me to relax and enjoy my vacation. Little did they know that the round trip to the post office for my expensive but useless phone call took about two hours. By the time I got back, Edith and my sons-in-law would have just finished a couple of rounds of tennis. It would be too hot to get in one more game. It was already time for lunch. My morning routine left me with a curiously empty feeling: a wake-up call. I decided that this was it. I had been with Hill & Knowlton for thirty-four years, half of my life, the last ten years as CEO—an unusually long tenure in our business. I felt I was beginning to stagnate in that role. I was 62, I felt great, I was ready for a new challenge, I was ready to give something back.

Upon returning to New York, I informed Don Johnston that I had decided to retire; I felt it was the right time to leave. We had just completed a strategic plan emphasizing new technologies and specializations. Under my stewardship, H&K had experienced ten years of unprecedented growth and diversification while maintaining its prestige and unique position in our field. The JWT Group chairman made a case for me to stay on until December 31, 1986, to ease the transition. I was reluctant, but on thinking it over began to see the positive side of delaying my departure; I had a whole year to prepare myself for the next phase of my life. The question of who should be my successor was quickly resolved. It seemed that Bob Dillenschneider, an eighteen-year H&K veteran based in Chicago who headed up our national division, had been lobbying the members of the JWT Board for the job, and they were already lined up behind him. I did suggest that there should at least be a choice, and that consideration should be given to other candidates, such as Fred Berger, another senior executive, but Don had his mind made up. Apparently it was not up to me to decide. Bob Dillenschneider would be H&K's next CEO.

In considering my retirement options, I set out on a re-search project serving just one client, namely, me. I began by systematically contacting half a dozen recently retired CEOs to ask for their advice: how had *they* handled their retirement, and what mistakes should I avoid? Some were still active on corporate boards; others had put money into investment vehicles and were actively managing their assets. And some had retired near a golf course or to a rocking chair on some southern porch. I had not anticipated, however, that I would receive a near unanimous recommendation: Do Not Make The Mistake Of Too Many Commitments. I listened carefully and then quickly fell into the trap of doing just that. I promptly signed up for an assortment of extracurricular projects that sounded appealing and wound up taking up far too much of my time. In the end I had to acknowledge the wisdom of one of my sources, who had told me that most executives looking at retirement dread finding themselves unemployed; "It's like a castration complex."

A friend of mine, Ed Block, AT&T's Public Relations Director, had also just retired. We had always hit it off; now we put our heads together to think up ways to join forces and use our time productively. Ed had joined with another retired PR director, Victor MacDonald of IBM, and set up a consultancy, the Block-Macdonald partnership. I joined their group, together with Stephen Stamas of Exxon, but gave it up a couple of years later. I woke up one day to the realization that this was precisely the kind of commitment I had been warned against. A client had insisted that I attend an early morning meeting in D.C., and as I was booking my pre-dawn flight, I suddenly asked myself, "What am I doing? I'm supposed to be retired!"

A more ambitious project I undertook with Ed Block was far longer lasting. It was an idea I had been mulling over for a while: what if we set up an institute to train American executives of multinational corporations in some of the skill sets I had found to be so sorely lacking for all these years? How many times hadn't I complained about the dearth of language and cultural understanding manifested by some of their top managers? It was time to do something about it. There should be a systematic approach for executives to learn what was going on outside their own borders, how to behave in a foreign culture, and how to cope with corporate problems arising abroad.

I mobilized a small group of enthusiasts, including David Gergen, at the time an editor at *U.S. News and World Report*, and Frank Stanton, the former President of CBS, with whom I served on two other boards. I laid out the plan: the Global Public Affairs Institute would be an independent, non-profit entity associated with one of the world's top universities. I felt it was important to have an academic connection in order to establish that it was a bona fide program, with input from academia as well as from business. We would offer seminars and conferences for senior management in public affairs and communication, led by experts in the field. The Institute would be financed by the multinational corporations using our services. Our first port of call was Harvard. We had two days of constructive meetings, at the end of which the Harvard professors promised to send us an outline of a prospective program. The proposal, when it arrived, came with major sticker shock. The price tag was quite unrealistic.

Next we approached New York University. It felt as if we were going from Tiffany's to Macy's, for NYU did not yet carry the prestige it has today. However, John Brademas, NYU's President, was immediately enthusiastic about the concept, especially since it would be the university's first interdisciplinary effort, bringing together historians, economists, political scientists, sociologists, and so on. We envisaged a curriculum that would include everything from economics to media studies and international politics, with the aim of giving the participants valuable exposure to the world beyond the United States. We had no trouble finding sponsors: many major corporations signed on, including AT&T, Boeing, Citicorp, Exxon, General Electric, Johnson & Johnson, Cigna, Rockwell, Bristol-Myers and General Motors. I was the chairman; Ed Block was the first president. James Armstrong of AT&T and later Bill Koplowitz of Citibank were our Executive Directors.

In its first decade the project was a great success. A cooperative arrangement with the European Centre for Public Affairs at Oxford University resulted in two jointly sponsored seminars at Oxford in 1991 and 1992. When budget cuts became the order of the day, however, some member companies withdrew their support, and in the early 2000s we had to call it a day.

In 1975 Mark Shubart, the President of Lincoln Center Institute, the educational arm of Lincoln Center, asked me to join his board. I was impressed with Mark's approach, a good mix of vision and pragmatism. I remained on that board for over 30 years; it was the only nonprofit board on which I served for an entire generation. I was especially taken with the leadership of Sandra Priest Rose, the board chair. Among the many chairmen I have ever come across, Mrs. Rose stood out for her leadership skills. She was a member of the philanthropic Rose family, New York real estate tycoons whose support of the city's educational and cultural life had had a significant impact. The Institute pioneered a new kind of intensive aesthetic education program in the schools, since research had shown that teenagers educated in the visual and performing arts were better-than-average students. After the successful introduction of "Imagination" as a learning tool in the schools, Edith and I came up with the idea of starting a competitive award program for New York's public schools, *The Imagination Award*. The $5000 prize would go to the school with the most creative program. Our first winner was a school on the lower East Side largely populated by kids from disadvantaged or dysfunctional family backgrounds. The school's remarkable headmistress had instituted a curriculum featuring Latin and sign language as the two required foreign languages. Another year we chose a school that had focused on all aspects of Egypt's ancient and modern history. A talented young student had composed an opera about Egypt, which was produced with the assistance of two members of the Metropolitan Opera staff. In my fifty-year experience with educational issues I have learned that strong leadership at the top of a school makes all the difference. It is the most important contributor to the development of the skills of our young.

I have sat on sixteen philanthropic boards in all, and with the exception of Lincoln Center, have made it a rule never to stay longer than four years. I was a popular recruit, because in enlisting me, the foundations expected to obtain indispensible PR advice on attracting new donors and keeping longtime contributors. At the initial meeting it was invariably made clear that I would be expected to direct more press exposure to the organization, and better publicity. I would humbly respond that my expertise also lay in other areas of consulting, and that I was afraid I might not meet their expectations, but they rarely heard me.

As I grew older, I became conscious of being drawn back to my Dutch roots. Gradually my old Dutch skin came to grow an extra layer over my newer American self. I felt rootless, aware of my divided loyalties. I would not describe it as a struggle as such, but I observed myself spending time following the political developments in the Netherlands as I had not done when I was Dutch, with a new interest in soccer matches. I also looked forward to our visits to Holland. Yet after three of four days back in my country of birth, I always felt that I'd had enough. The place was too confining, too depressing. What was it that was engrained deeply in my skin, I wondered—my Dutch roots, or the adoption of an American persona? Or had I become a mongrel, impossible to define?

Some of my board activities were directly related to those Dutch roots. Edith was involved with the Anne Frank Foundation, and we were both drawn into an initiative to promote Dutch-American cultural and educational ex-changes. I learned that in 1921 five Americans of Dutch descent had come together in New York's Century Club to found the Netherland-America Foundation (NAF), in order to "strengthen cultural ties between the United States and the Netherlands." The founders had included Franklin D. Roosevelt, a young and upcoming politician at the time, whose calling card read "Librarian of Hyde Park, New York," In successive years, the Society was led by such luminaries as Commerce Secretary William Redfield, IBM's Thomas Watson, and Charles Scribner. By the mid-century, however, with little money available to support its mission, it had largely gone dormant.

In 1989, we resuscitated it by merging two struggling organizations, the Netherlands-America Community Association and the Dutch-American West India Company Foundation, into one. I became the new NAF's first postwar chairman. It wasn't easy for our organization to gain a foothold on the New York philanthropic scene. We appealed to new arrivals from the Netherlands for support, but these were not particularly interested in causes related to the motherland.[13] It was a question of neglect rather than denial. Integrating into America was a priority for them; besides, Social-Democratic Holland was not accustomed to private charitable giving. Undaunted, we began to sponsor exchanges in the arts and postgraduate education. Today

---

13 I was amused to read the following observation by the Columbia University Professor A.J. Barnouw who from 1921 to 1960 wrote a *Monthly Letter* for the NAF: "Publicity is a state of exposure that the Hollander shuns rather than seeks, and he finds something indecent and impertinent in the request of a publisher that he should write his own life story." (1938)

the NAF has grown into a mature, well-funded organization with a wide range of programs through its branches in half a dozen American cities.

One of my tasks as NAF chairman was to go to JFK airport to greet Princess Margriet, daughter of Queen Beatrix of the Netherlands, upon her arrival to attend the Peter Stuyvesant Ball, our primary fundraiser. The Princess was, and still is, the foundation's Royal Patron, and always came with a retinue composed of her husband Pieter van Vollenhoven, two or more children, a lady-in-waiting, and two Dutch security officers. The thought that our philanthropic institution, always short of money, was expected to pick up the hotel tab for the whole entourage gave rise to some irritation on my part, although at least KLM picked up the cost of the air travel. More annoying was the need to trek to the airport twice in a row when the royal couple decided to come in on separate flights. To make matters worse, the consort had a habit of lecturing me on American politics on our way back to the city. It was enough to make an anti-royalist of me.

My other new ties with Holland were focused on music. A friend asked me to help set up an American "Friends of the Amsterdam Concertgebouw Orchestra." To support the purchase of much-needed new instruments, we organized a dinner for symphony lovers when the orchestra came to play at Carnegie Hall. The orchestra enjoyed a first class reputation, but did not come to the States often enough to make it as popular as the Berlin or Vienna philharmonics, which made more frequent pilgrimages to New York.

Our weekend house in Sheffield was just a short half-hour drive from Tanglewood, the summer home of the Boston Symphony Orchestra. We were regular attendees of its music festival. It struck us that the Tanglewood school for advanced young musicians counted many foreigners from abroad, but none from the Netherlands. I decided to remedy that situation by getting the BSO to agree to establish an audition center in Holland. Once the BSO was on board, I persuaded the Dutch Ministry of Culture to foot the bill. For a few years a group of eminent American musicians would fly to Holland for the auditions, including the famed soprano Phyllis Curtin. That first year I introduced the group to a genuine Indonesian *rijsttafel* during a break in the audition schedule. In 2011, after the World Trade Center attacks, the annual winter trip was cancelled, and the program was never revived. Edith and I, however, have continued to sponsor Tanglewood Fellows from the Netherlands, resulting in some wonderful friendships with talented musicians.

Our daughters and their husbands produced five grandchildren for us to adore. Since one of our daughters lived in London with her family, the most effective way to get the whole clan together was for me to bribe them by renting an attractive house somewhere in the Caribbean, Provence, Martha's Vineyard, or Tuscany. The offer of a holiday in a sunny location proved irresistible for children and grandchildren alike. Our most memorable rental, in my view, was the one in Lambesc, an ancient capital of Provence. The villa had a tennis court, swimming pool, a court for playing *boules* and a servant from Burkina Faso who made us drinks and ironed my underwear, and told us he dreamed of emigrating to America. I cloistered myself in the library, immersed in the villa's books and World Wars I and II memorabilia—a genuine war museum. The owner of the house was the son of Paul Reynaud, France's last prime minister before France's surrender to Germany in June 1940. A large portrait of Prime Minister Clemenceau, Reynaud's political sponsor in the first World War, hung over the mantelpiece. Signed photographs of Reynaud with Churchill, Eden and de Gaulle, most taken between September 1939 and June 1940, were displayed on the walls and on the desk. The library contained an extensive collection of books and leather-bound magazines cataloguing the history of the early and mid-Twentieth Century. In 1940 Reynaud, after refusing to sign the armistice, had tried to flee from Paris ahead of the invading German army. His car, loaded with luggage on top, had veered off the road and hit a tree. His mistress, a countess, was killed on the spot. Reynaud was injured and delivered by Marshal Pétain to the Germans, who incarcerated him in a prison camp until liberation.

Retirement was a time for reflection about the past. While I'd been working, I had been too busy to think much about my early years. I had always looked forward; now I finally had the leisure to look back. Edith had been busy transcribing her diaries and her parents' letters, with a view to turning them into a book. I too was inspired to put pen to paper, and try to make sense of what happened to me all those years ago. One night, at the home of friends in Santa Fe, our hosts prompted me to tell them about my life during and after the war. For several hours I held the floor.

Our friends strongly encouraged me to write it all down. A light bulb went on. Edith and I had been thinking that writing down our experiences would be for our grandchildren to know our stories. Maybe there was a wider audience out there for the stories we had to tell.

Writing my memoir became a stop-and-go effort, spread over several years. At first we'd had the idea of writing a joint memoir, alternating Edith's experiences with mine. But we had to abandon that approach—our stories did not mesh closely enough. Edith had her documents to refer to—the letters and diaries. I had only my long-suppressed memories. In the 1980s, when I began working on *Long Way Back to the River Kwai*, there were still relatively few accounts of the POW experience in Asia; the Pacific theater had taken a back seat to the war in Europe. It is only recently that there has been renewed interest in the war experiences of the likes of me.

It was a slow start; it took me a while to "peel the layers of the onion," as my daughter put it. At the end it turned into a sprint. I was conscious of my late friend Max Weisglas's philosophical pronouncement when we visited him before he died. "We are now sitting in the very last compartment of the train," he said.

Even now, the memories of World War II have not faded away. Our bookshelves are laden with volumes about the Holocaust, the German invasion and occupation, the Pacific War and the Japanese conquest of South East Asia. Edith still mourns the parents and brother she lost to the Nazis. I too think more and more often of my parents and the dead friends from my prison days. I have even grown a little more mellow about the Japanese; they have earned my respect for their stoicism in the face of centuries of earthquakes and tsunamis, and, more recently, nuclear disaster. At the same time I cannot help but keep a wary eye on them. When I learned that in 2013 Prime Minister Abe won his electoral victory on a strong nationalist platform, and that he allowed three members of his cabinet to make a pilgrimage to the Yasukuni shrine honoring many WWII war criminals, I felt discouraged. Tens of millions Japanese apparently still hold the view that their country was the victim, and not the aggressor, in the events that led to Pearl Harbor.

We eventually gave up our apartment in New York City. With age, our ties to the City had loosened. Friends had moved away; some (too many) had died. After twenty-three moves in sixty-five years of marriage, we took stock. Where did we want to spend the rest of our days? The answer was: in Sheffield. We feel deeply rooted in the Berkshires, the house on the lake where we gather our extended clan around us as often as we can.

Even while writing my book, I still had plenty of time to sit on non-profit boards. One of the last, and most satisfying, was Bennington College, under the forward-thinking leadership of my friend President Liz Coleman and Board Chair Deborah Wadsworth. I found the board meetings with those two dynamic people at the helm extremely stimulating; they seemed in turn to appreciate my attempts to find solutions to some of the knotty issues the college was facing.

In 2013, a few years after we sold our New York apartment, I gave up my last non-profit board chairmanship.

When I announced my resignation, I heard a polite, probably insincere, murmur of regret. Having just passed my ninetieth birthday, I informed my colleagues that I remembered proposing that board memberships should end at age seventy-five or eighty. I had obviously overstayed my own welcome.

My friendship with Harold Burson, an icon of the PR industry, has lasted into our nineties. Harold was the co-founder of Burson-Marsteller, which some years ago overtook Hill & Knowlton as the largest PR firm in the world. We have lunch once or twice a year, bemoaning the fact that we would not have a chance of being hired in today's world. We like to kid each other about our erstwhile rivalry. Harold, now in his nineties, still goes to the office every day. He too is nostalgic for the days when CEOs of large corporations and government leaders used to call him in for advice. That time is gone. The PR business of today no longer means policy advice; it's all "transactional" now. These days, PR firms are expected to produce films, videos, digital materials, and exploit social media. If we were working today, we would be dealing with midlevel client executives wrestling with more prosaic problems, instead of having the ear of the top brass.

Good fortune has brought me many blessings and benefits. None are greater than Edith, the love of my life. We have been together for over 66 years. She was of the generation of dutiful wives who followed their husbands. In doing so, she made sacrifice after sacrifice. The roving nature of my job prevented her from finishing her studies in Amsterdam, and then Geneva, and then London. When we ultimately landed in New York, she was finally able to finish her studies, completing a Masters degree in Gerontology at Columbia University. To me, her greatest talent is her ability to cement the solid bonds by which she has kept the members of our family together. We are all consummate defenders of each other. Over the years our children have become our best friends.

In 1997 *Edith's Story* was published, in a Dutch translation of the original English text. The book took off immediately. It was published in nine languages, including Japanese and Chinese, won two literary prizes, had many reprints and excellent reviews in dozens of prominent publications around the world. It is still keeping Edith busy with interviews, talks and panel discussions. My own book *Long Way Back to the River Kwai* came out a few years later; it too was well reviewed and published abroad, but not to the extent that Edith's was. I liked to tease her that after all the years of living in my shadow as the corporate wife, the roles were now reversed; I was now the helpmeet carrying her briefcase.

In 2013 we received a visit from Karel Dahmen, whom I had not seen in seventy-three years. In May 1940 he had been one of my companions on our flight from Holland aboard the vessel *Zeemanshoop (Seaman's Hope)*. Karel, four years my senior and a self-confessed rather inexperienced sailor, had been our skipper, standing at the helm of the small coastguard boat we had hijacked on the day Holland capitulated. During the fraught 26-hour crossing over mine-laden waters, we hadn't had much chance to get to know each other. Now, of the 46 people on board, we are the only two left alive. Karel, after a successful, peripatetic life, also wound up living in the U.S.—in Austin, Texas. We find that we have a lot in common and we enjoy each other's company tremendously.

In May 2015, both Karel and I crossed the Atlantic back to Scheveningen to mark the 75th anniversary of the *Seaman's Hope* crossing. A major commemoration of the event had been organized. It had all started with an email from Bill Forster, an Englishman whose father had been an officer on HMS *Venomous*, the British Navy destroyer that had picked us up in the middle of the North Sea as we were trying to reach England. Forster had become interested in the story of the *Seaman's Hope* when doing the research for a history of his father's ship *(A Hard Fought Ship)*. After finding me through links to my first book, Forster wrote that he had found a copy of an old naval chart on the back of which we had scribbled the names of the refugees aboard the *Seaman's Hope*. Bill had set up a website, and through the dogged sleuthing of the Dutch historian and journalist Wout Smit, the family members, children and grandchildren of most of the passengers who had been my traveling companions were tracked down. Forster wrote:

The starting point for my research into the story of the Zeemanshoop *was the photograph of its passengers on the deck of HMS* Venomous *taken by Lt Peter Kershaw RNVR. They were smartly dressed and looked as if they were on a theatre outing or going shopping rather than fleeing for their lives. This photograph made me want to find out what happened to them after they landed at Dover that evening— and in their subsequent lives.*

Thanks to Forster's enthusiasm, the story took on a life of its own. A Dutch journalist, Danny Verbaan, wrote a book about our escape entitled *Weg (Away)*. The original *Zeemanshoop* was found; the plucky lifeboat, decommissioned in 1976, had been bought by a group of enthusiasts who were working to restore her to her original condition. I was assured that she would be shipshape in time for the commemoration.

And so, on the morning of May 14, 2015, exactly 75 years to the day after we had jumped aboard the *Zeemanshoop* and made our escape, I climbed the steep staircase to the fisherman's auction house at the far end of Scheveningen Harbor and looked down on that very vessel, docked in the exact same spot where we had boarded her so many years ago. It was an emotional moment for me, and an eye-opener: I could not get over how that modest little boat could possibly have held forty-six souls.

It was the beginning of a day-long commemoration. Over a hundred dignitaries and family members showed up for the event, some from as far away as Australia. The British Navy had found the event sufficiently important to send over a war ship. There were speeches from the British Ambassador and the Mayor of The Hague, as well as Karel Dahmen and myself. The media were there in full force. I found myself pursued by cameras and journalists demanding a window of time to interview me. *Here I am, finally getting a taste of what it's like to be hounded by paparazzi!* I thought to myself.

A naval engineer, the son of one of the students who had taken control of the boat, told us that our survival had been a miracle. The boat had sat far too low in the water; any sudden move or rough wave would have caused it to capsize. Good weather and an unusually calm North Sea had been our saving grace. He also explained that our amateur crew had set the compass north-west, which, even if by some piece of luck the tides had not swept us through the Straits of Dover out into the Atlantic Ocean, would probably have dashed us to pieces on England's rocky shore. Finally, he said that when the British ship spotted us, we had failed to identify ourselves. "Rather than taking a chance, a less humane British commander could simply have blown the unidentified vessel out of the water."

The highlight of that memorable day was when we were taken for a spin around the harbor in the restored *Zeemanshoop*: the crew, Karel and I, and the unshakable throng of print, television and radio journalists. We were no more than twenty on board, but it was very crowded. We could not imagine that there had been forty-six of us on that foolhardy journey; there wasn't enough room for even half of that number to sit down.

Once again I was struck by the brave, desperate decision of our fellow passengers, strangers to one another, to shut the door of their homes at a moment's notice, leaving family, friends, colleagues and all worldly goods behind, only to entrust their lives to a group of inexperienced boys and sail into an uncertain future. I told the assembled crowd that we should not forget the many thousands of refugees, displaced persons and boat people who continue every day to risk their lives on overcrowded, dangerously unseaworthy ships for a chance at freedom. It appears that history will never stop repeating itself.

The celebration also opened my eyes to the trickiness of perspective. My experiences as a POW of the Japanese in the years after my escape from Holland had always overshadowed, even eclipsed, this first taste of war. In thinking back on the war, I had never allowed myself to dwell on the implications of this first risky adventure. Grateful as I am for my many narrow escapes and subsequent 75 years of relative peace and tranquility as a citizen of the free Western world, I realize that it is the combination of both of those war experiences that have colored who I am.

I would like to think that the world is still my oyster. The thought may no longer be based on the reality of our current circumstances. We continue to travel, but less extensively than before. The interests remain constant; the passion has faded. Age imposes its own immutable limitations. My parents, my cousin Dick who had made the *Zeemanshoop* crossing with me, John Hill and a few others remain sharply etched in my mind. I could sketch them for you if only I knew how to draw. By contrast, the memories of the many faces I encountered over the course of my long career and retirement are faint in color and contour.

A week after the May 14 festivities in Scheveningen, Karel Dahmen, traveling in Europe, called to say that although he had enjoyed all the fuss and attention paid to our big adventure, he felt it was enough now: time to leave all that behind. "Let's plan for the future," he suggested optimistically. I admire his attitude.

Both Edith and I have retained our positive outlook and our belief in the adage that the elderly should keep busy as long as they can. At the same time we recognize that, at least so far, we have beaten the odds. I sometimes wonder what new challenge may come along. And whether I would want to or be able to respond to it.

Contentment now is the realization that the slowdown of age is compensated for by a greater awareness and enjoyment of our immediate environment: the songs of the birds, the fullness of our blooming garden, the views of the mountain and the pond with its egrets, geese, swans and eagles, and the splendor of the colors in the rising morning sun and fading evening light.

* * *

INDEX

FURTHER READING

Foster, William, *The Voyage of the Zeemans Hoop*, http://www.holywellhousepublishing.co.uk/Zeemanshoop_voyage.html
http://www.holywellhousepublishing.co.uk/anniversary2.html

Hill, John W., *The Making of a Public Relations Man*, David McKay, 1963

Trento, Susan B., *The Power House: Robert Keith Gray and the Selling of Access and Influence in Washington*, St. Martin's Press, 1992

Velmans, Edith, *Edith's Story*, Soho Press, 1999/van Horton Books, 2014

Velmans, Loet, *Long Way Back to the River Kwai*, Arcade, 2003

After surviving many narrow escapes during World War II and winding up a prisoner of war of the Japanese in Asia, Loet Velmans made his way from his native Holland to America with his young family. Starting as a young executive in the New York based public relations firm Hill & Knowlton, he was sent to Paris to establish a presence for the firm in Europe and eventually the rest of the world; in doing so he had to grapple with having to do business with his former Japanese captors. He was eventually called back to New York to become his firm's Chairman and CEO. Upon retiring, he turned to writing; his war memoir, *Long Way Back to the River Kwai*, was hailed as a valuable contribution to the history of the war in the Pacific. His wife, Edith Velmans, is the author of the acclaimed *Edith's Story*. They live by a lake in Sheffield, Massachusetts.

Made in United States
Orlando, FL
21 December 2024

56320434R00155